SHE THANKED HIM

Olive Gardiner

CRIMOND
HOUSE

Published in 2012 by
Crimond House Publications
A division of Ards Evangelical Bookshop
"Crimond House"
48 Frances Street
Newtownards
Co. Down
BT23 7DN
www.crimondhouse.com

Printed in Glasgow by Bell & Bain Ltd.
Cover design by Martin Kenny. www.martinkenny.co.uk
Typesetting by Crimond House Publications.

ISBN: 978 1 908618 02 3

Acknowledgments

It is thirty-one years since my first book was published entitled "She Touched Him." This one is probably my final book of poems. I am calling it "She Thanked Him" as I have so much for which to thank God. This volume contains all of the poems I have been enabled to write over the years.

My thoughts return to the late Mr. Stewart McVittie who was the first to encourage me to put my early poems into print. Also I am grateful to my mother who "sent" me to elocution lessons. She was the instrument the Lord used to accomplish His plan for my life in later years.

There have been many along the way who have encouraged me to keep writing, Christian Endeavour comrades, members of the Presbyterian and Methodist Women's Associations and other groups in the many churches where I have been graciously received and made to feel at home. There are also many of my friends I want to thank, but it is impossible to name them all.

My family has supported me throughout my "writing journey" and I would particularly like to thank my son-in-law, the Rev. Stephen Greasley, who has made use of my books in his ministry and has made many encouraging suggestions which have been very helpful.

Most of all I thank and praise my Father, God, for all His leading and guiding throughout the years. Every poem has been rooted in His Word. May all who read them know His rich blessing in their lives.

Additional thanks must go to Ricky McCoubrey of Crimond House Publications who so graciously allowed me to have a part in the preparation of this book.

Contents

She Thanked Him

She Thanked Him

Luke 2:36-38

Anna, widowed very young, chose of her own accord
To spend her days in worship, fasting, praying to the Lord.
The Temple was her only home 'til she was eighty-four,
A Prophetess, her calling, she knew God's plan held more.
And so, she waited patiently until that one great day
When Jesus was presented and she heard old Simeon pray;
She heard him praise the Sovereign Lord and thank Him
                                                    for His peace.
He called the baby, in his arms, a 'Light' that would not
cease.
Anna was overjoyed to hear old Simeon's song of praise.
She thanked the Lord she'd seen the Child, God's Son,
                                                    in her old age.
She spoke His name to all around saying, "the Christ has
come."
She'd lived her life for Him alone, now He would call her
home.

All For Him

Mark 12:41-44

The temple courts were thronged with rich and poor
Coming and going through the treasury door,
The poor, offering their alms without delay,
The rich, with many servants making way,
Sounding their coming, so that all might see
How much they gave ---- their generosity.

Among the jostling crowds a woman crept,
Trying to hide, she almost lost her step,
Wearing dark clothes and sorrowful of face.
She clutched her shawl and hurried on apace,
Two copper coins were gripped within her fist,
All that she had, ---- to God she made her gift.

Jesus had noted the widow's sacrifice.
He knew her circumstances, knew her life,
He knew her sorrows, knew her loneliness,
Her hopes and fears, her joys and her distress.
He turned to His disciples with this word,
"The rich gave some --- she gave Me all she had."

Yes, out of her poverty she gave her all,
Nothing held back, all given to the Lord.
The ostentatious rich had given a part
Only to boost their pride, not from the heart.
Our Saviour gave His all to save from sin
Those who repent and give their all to Him.

Beyond the Babe

God, manifest in flesh, came as a babe to earth;
Jesus, His given name, a child of holy birth.
A stable sheltered Him from cold, a manger cradled Him,
Immanuel, God with us, came to save the world from sin.

A boy grew up in Nazareth and played with other boys,
He worked beside his father, He brought his mother joy,
He learned to fashion tables, to carve beauty out of wood,
His neighbours watched and wondered at this young boy
doing good.

When he was twelve his parents took him to Jerusalem
To celebrate Passover with the other boys and men.
They found him in the temple, sitting among the wise;
"I must be in my Father's house," he said, to their surprise.

Jesus grew to manhood, left his mother's side and home.
With chosen friends He healed the sick, His message was,
'Just come.'
"Come unto me, you weary, and I will give you rest,"
"Come unto me, you thirsty," and they came at his behest.

Three years was all that Jesus had to teach about God's love.
Crowds followed in his footsteps and watched His every
move.
But sin and jealously and pride soon nailed Him to a tree;
Love died that day upon a hill, to set all sinners free.

The Babe of Bethlehem is our Lord, that Boy, the Son of
God.
That Man, Immanuel, God with us, our Saviour on the
cross,
Is now enthroned at God's right hand, His work on earth is
done;
And one day soon, His word is sure, He's promised to re-
turn.

Burden Bearing

In Seattle, 'Olympics' for children took place;
These children were special, from every race.
All were disabled in various ways
But determined to give of their best on the day.
Nine children lined up for the hundred yards dash,
Tummies were churning and hearts beating fast.

The starting gun sounded,the children set off,
The audience cheered from the grandstand aloft.
When they came to a corner a little boy slipped
And lay on the ground, so ashamed that he'd tripped.
The others looked back and stopped dead in the race,
Turned back to the child with tears staining his face.
A girl, with Downs Syndrome, bent down to her friend,
Placed a kiss on his cheek, wiped his tears with her dress.

With arms linked together they all started to run,
When they got to the tape it was judged that all won.
In the stands people wept as thy stood up to cheer,
Not one person there was ashamed of his tears.
The children, disabled in body and mind,
Had shown love to their friend, what it meant to be kind!
'Bear the burdens of others,' is God's will for us,
Help someone who's hurting without any fuss,
Speak a word to encourage, say a prayer for their needs,
Then God's love and God's mercy will bless you indeed.

This is from a real life story.

But You Would Not

Matthew 23:37

Wrapped in the golden sun, it's walls agleam,
The city lay, spread out ----- Jerusalem.
Large crowds of pilgrims filled the dusty streets,
Some riding donkeys, others on sore feet.
Rich men and beggars jostled by noisy crowds,
Street vendors, crying their wares aloud,
Families and friends , the greatest and the least
Thronging the city for the holy feast.

Jesus looked out upon that careless throng
Unconscious of it's need, it's sin and wrong,
And in His heavy sorrow wept hot tears
For those whose eyes were blind, who had deaf ears.
His heart was broken by their guilt and sin,
Their lack of love for others and for Him,
The evil in their hearts that sin had wrought;
And over them He wept --- "I would -- but you would not."
Yes, Jesus wept over fair Jerusalem;
For man's indifference to his need of Him.
He longed to gather men into His arms
Just as a hen gathers her chicks from harm.
But men stretched out those arms upon a tree
And left Him hanging there , in agony,
Dying for men ,the evil they had wrought;
"I would have given you life --- but you would not."

The Saviour is still reaching out His arms
Seeking to save the lost from sin and harm.
Have you responded to the Saviour's call
And given your life to Him Who gave His all?
Or, are you still refusing Him Who died
To save you from your sin, -- The Crucified --
Who still weeps for the evil you have wrought;
And still says, "I would --- but you would not."

Closed Doors

John 20:19

Their Lord was dead – hanged on a Roman cross!
His followers, scared, heart- broken at His loss
Had shut themselves away behind closed doors,
Afraid of what the Jews might have in store
For them; ashamed that they had fled
And left their Lord alone ---- now He was dead.

Their Lord was dead. Of that they were quite sure.
Then,who was this who entered through closed doors?
"Peace be to you", He said; their fears were stilled.
"Look, see my hands and side." Their souls were thrilled.
"Peace be to you," it really was His voice,
 He was alive and with Him they rejoiced.
Closed doors! Shut in with all our fears,
The future without hope, blinded by tears;
The Lord seems dead to us, our sufferings great,
Existence ordered by a cruel fate,
And then, Christ comes, no doors can keep Him out,
His words of peace remove our fears and doubts
The Living Lord resides within our souls
Bringing us peace and joy, making us whole.

Come

Our lives are bound by daily regulations.
The morning comes, we rise, we make decisions.
Will we have tea and toast or 'Special K?'
We live our lives, make choices everyday,
What will we eat? What will we drink?
Our minds are cluttered, we can hardly think!
Yet, there is One Who calls, "Come unto Me,
Come unto Me, you thirsty, it is free,
Drink of the water and find life anew,
I paid the price. My life I gave for you."
        Isaiah 55:1

The days pass by, demands claim all our time,
Work, family, friends, problems and joys; we find
Few moments for ourselves to rest, relax,
Burdens pile up, stresses and strains attack.
So taken up with all the world holds dear
We lose our souls, our lives are lived with fears.
There's One Who stands beside us through our day
"Come, come unto Me ye weary", hear Him say,
"Come, heavy laden one I'll give you rest,
I'm waiting now for you, I know what's best."
        Matthew 11:28ff

Many are thirsty, but they don't know why!
Days filled with pleasures, nothing satisfies.
At Sychar's well a woman met the Christ,
She heard of Living Water for her thirst
And ran into her village, calling, "Come,
Come meet with One who knows all I have done."
Many, who heard her words came to the Lord,
Believed His message, trusted in His word.
Do we invite our friends to meet the Christ?
Do we say, "Come, and He will change your life?"
        John 4:29

Continued

'Come now , for all is ready,' is the word.
The host invites us all, He is the Lord.
He's sent His servants out to say, "It's time;"
Time for salvation's feast, for yours and mine.
Have you accepted? Have you said, "Yes , Lord?"
Or are you still refusing His true word?
He's calling still; you're precious in His sight,
Come, follow Him, He'll make you His delight.
> Luke 14:17

The Spirit and the bride say , "Come",
Whoever is thirsty, let him come.
And whoever wishes, let him take the free gift
Of the water of life.
> Revelation 20

David

1 Samuel 17

How had it happened? I was just a lad
Standing on a hillside, facing great Goliath.
I'd only come from home to bring supplies.
My brothers were the soldiers but their cries
Of fear just made me feel ashamed
The God of Israel, my God, was thus defamed.

Because I wanted to extol His name
I said that I would fight the Philistine.
Saul wanted me to wear a sword and shield
But I refused, my sling and stones I'd wield
As once I'd done against the lion and the bear
And with God's help had killed the hungry pair.

I took my staff and sling and five smooth stones
And then approached the mighty Philistine.
He watched me as I hurried down the hill,
Then laughed and jeered at me as I stood still.
"Your flesh will feed the great birds of the air
Come here," he yelled, as I stood trembling there.

I knew that God was with me in this fight,
 That facing down this Philistine was right.
"I come against you in the name of God
Whose armies you've insulted by your words;
This day the Lord will give your head to me
And all will see His mighty victory."

Goliath, angered by the things I'd said,
Lifted his heavy sword and unafraid
Moved out to meet me as I took a stone
And placed it in my sling, then, as I ran,
I swung it round and round, aimed at Goliath's head —
And lo, the giant Philistine dropped dead.

Continued

The soldiers of the God of Israel pursued
The enemy; a great victory ensued.
God's name was honoured there in every tent.
Saul sought to honour me, but I'd been sent
By Israel's God Who gave me strength to win
So all the glory goes direct to Him.

Don't Cry

Luke 7:11-17

"Don't cry," Jesus said to the widow of Nain
As He looked , with compassion on this woman's pain.
Her precious companion, her dear son was dead,
Her only support in that coffin was laid.
Her friends gathered round as they walked to the grave,
The heart broken widow tried hard to be brave.

Who was this stranger who said, "Do not cry"
Whose voice was so gentle, had such love in His eye?
The crowd became silent, had nothing to say
As the stranger approached the cortege on it's way.
He bent over the coffin and stretched out His hand,
Then spoke to the dead man in tones of command.

" Young man, I say unto you, 'Arise.'
The mourners all gasped and looked on in surprise
As the young man sat up and started to talk;
Jesus took the man's hand and they started to walk
To the grief stricken widow whose tears turned to joy
When the Lord, in compassion, had raised up her boy.

God looks with compassion on us in our grief.
He binds up our wounds and brings us relief.
He whispers, "Don't cry" and dries all our tears.
His arms are around us, He calms every fear.
For God knows what it's like to bear sorrow and loss,
He gave His own Son to death on the cross.

Face to Face

One night, in the midst of a terrible storm,
A child and his father, looking very forlorn,
Booked into an inn, got a dark bedroom,
Because of the storm only lit by the moon.
All was so strange the small boy was afraid
As he lay in the gloom, his dad by his side.

Outside the inn the wild wind seemed to call;
Shadows cast by the moon moved over the walls.
The child shuddered, then spoke,"Are you there , Dad?"
                                    he cried,
"Is your face turned towards me? It's so dark, I'm afraid."
"You're safe, I can see you," was his father's reply,
"My face is towards you, sleep well, do not cry,"

Our Saviour lived through deep darkness as well
As He hung on the cross, His suffering was real;
For the face of His Father was turned from His Son
As He bore all our sin until it was done.
By His death on the cross Jesus gave God a face,
And that face towards us is always of grace.

Hannah

1 Samuel 1

I really was heartbroken, down, depressed.
Nothing had changed — year after year had passed
And still our home was empty --- not a sound
Of baby cries or toddler running round.
Elkanah did not understand, "My wife
Why do you weep? I love you more than life.
Don't I mean more to you than many sons?"
But yet my heart was sore, I mourned alone.

Year after year we all went up to Shiloh,
Myself, Elkanah, his other wife Penniah.
She had her family but poked fun at me
Making my childless state her victory.
Rejoicing when she saw my endless tears,
My loneliness,my sorrow,and my fears.
But then, that year I brought it all to God,
Poured out my longings there before the Lord.

To the Almighty God I made a vow.
If He, in love and mercy, would allow
Me, His servant, to have a baby son
Then I would give him back, while he was young,
To serve the Lord for all his future days;
To worship Him and follow all His ways.
In brokenness and tears I stood and prayed.
My prayers were quiet thoughts, whispered, not said.

Then suddenly, a voice, loud and unreal
Broke into my prayers --- I turned quite pale.
Eli,the priest, approached me with harsh words,
"Woman, you're drunk, you're state is quite absurd,
When will you stop the drinking of much wine?"
"Not so, my lord", I said, "That fault's not mine.
My heart was filled with misery and grief,
I've told it all to God and found His peace."

Continued

Eli then spoke to me in kinder tones.
"Return in peace, my child, unto your home.
May God, the God of Israel, grant you prayer
And keep you always in His loving care."
I dried my tears, my misery had gone;
We thanked the Lord and then set out for home.
I felt that God had heard my heart's request,
That He would answer when He knew it best.

The time did come. God's answer to my cry
Was Samuel, our precious baby boy. I named him thus.
It means 'asked of the Lord.'
My heart was filled with praise to know, that God,
The Holy One had seen my deep despair
And granted my request showing His care.
When he was weaned I gave him back to God
And he became a servant of the Lord.

Yes --- as I vowed --- I gave him back to God.
And I rejoiced and praised and thanked the Lord
Who'd heard my prayer and given me my boy.
I gave him back --- it gave me peace and joy;
The Lord was gracious unto me again.
My heart was filled to overflowing when
Five boys and girls became our family.
I gave God Samuel --- He poured His love on me.

Often we wait for answers to our prayers,
The years pass by with more and more grey hairs.
The heavens seem as brass, God's ears seem deaf,
And we feel all alone steeped in our grief.
But, as we see, God has His perfect plan,
And when we give our all into His hand
He works to perfect all of our concerns
And gives far more than that for which we yearned.

He Didn't Stay Dead

The teacher was telling the story
Of the death of the Christ to her class.
Little Japanese children were listening
To what was coming to pass.
A small boy jumped up
With a very loud cry:
"Not fair," "Not fair," he shouted,
"Not fair," Him was one swell Guy."
A little girl, sitting beside him
Pulled him down and patted his head,
"Don't get so upset," she whispered,
"For you see, He didn't stay dead!"

I Want To See The Queen

A little boy watched, at the palace gates,
The sentries, standing so tall and so straight.
The child was in rags, his bare feet were frozen
As he gazed at the soldier standing before him.
"Please, mister sentry,can you let me in.
I've come a long way to speak to the Queen?"

The soldier ignored the poor child at his feet
And marched up and down, very smart on his beat,
But the small boy persisted and put out his hand
And pulled at the leg of the very tall man.
"You must open the gates and let me go in,
Please mister, please sir, I must see the Queen."

Tears flowed down the face of the small, dirty boy,
And a small crowd of people gathered nearby.
They listened, as he continued to plead,
Unable to help this small child in need.
Then, a tall, bearded man appeared on the scene,
"Come with me son, you will see the Queen.."

The man took the boy's hand, they walked through the
gates,
The big doors were opened, no need to wait.
Down a long passage they walked, hand in hand,
Then came to a door which looked very grand.
The man knocked on it softly, a voice said, "Come in."
The little boy entered, and there sat the Queen!

Victoria lifted the child on to her knee;
"Tell me, my boy,why you've come to see me."
The little one told of his sick Mum at home,
Of his brothers and sisters whom he'd left all alone;
The Queen wiped his tears and tucked gold in his hand,
He climbed down from her knee but continued to stand.

Continued

"Thank you, oh thank you for what you have done,
But please, ma'am just tell me before I go home.
Who is the kind man who helped me today?
He just took my hand and showed me the way.
I'd like to say, 'thank you', for all he has done."
Victoria smiled at the child, "He's the Prince he's my son."

Prince George showed a boy the way to the Queen.
He entered her presence, was showed the way in.
Our Prince and our Saviour has shown us the way
To His Father , our God, Who is King of Kings.
We come to the Father through Jesus the Son,
And receive His salvation by what He has done.

It Came to Pass

Luke 22:54

Oh yes, I'd sworn that I would follow and not turn away.
I recall it all as if it happened yesterday.
I can picture yet the look of love on Jesus' face
When He, with gentle voice, told me I'd deny Him thrice.
And yet it came to pass.

I'd followed at a distance as the soldiers bound His wrists.
They pushed, then dragged Him roughly, to the house of
the High Priest.
I stood among the shadows, warmed myself by the log fire,
Forgetful of my Lord's forecast that I would lie.
Oh yes, it came to pass.

I've no excuse ---- I Peter, who'd professed my faithfulness,
Before a servant girl and under stress
 Denied, with oaths and curses, violent words that I knew
Him,
Had been His follower and friend.
Just as He'd said --- three times!
But yes it came to pass.

I did not know a cock could crow so loudly in the night --
The awful sound pierced through my heart – I turned to-
wards the light
And met the look of sorrow and of love the Master cast.
Oh yes, it came to pass.

I went into the dark, dark night, a helpless man,
Tears filled my eyes, my soul, my heart, as from that place I
ran.
They crucified my Saviour on a hill called Calvary.
I did not see Him suffer there but know it was for me.
Oh yes, it came to pass.

Continued

I went back to my boat, back to familiar ways,
But Jesus met me on the beach one day.
He'd said He'd rise again!
His overwhelming love was poured on me – the least of men.
Oh yes, it came to pass.

There on the beach He asked three times, "Peter do you love Me?"
My heart was broken by His words – His love had set me free.
"Go feed My sheep, go feed My lambs, go feed My sheep,
Go into all the world and be My witness."
Oh yes, it came to pass.

Majesty and Humility

Palm Sunday - Philippians 2

"Blessed is the King," they cried that day
As Jesus rode the donkey in the way.
They hailed Him with palm branches
                                waved around,
They even spread their garments on the
                                        ground,
Believing that He'd come to save their land
And save them from the Roman rulers' hands.

Oh yes, He was indeed the Mighty One;
He'd left His Kingdom, come to earth,
                                God's Son.
He'd taken on the form of humankind,
Become a servant, just with us in mind,
Seeking to save us all from death and loss.
He even let us nail Him to a cross !

The King of all the world upon a cross !
The sinless Son of God suffering for us!
His blood He shed to take away our sin
That, one day, we would reign in heaven
                                with Him.
The risen Saviour is at God's right hand.
The Blessed King who took the form of
                                        man.

My Redeemer Liveth

Job 19:25

What words of faith and confidence are these
Spoken by Job, God's servant, on his knees;
Brought low by loss and pain and suffering,
Scorned by his neighbours, criticised by friends,
Searching for God amid his deep despair,
Seeking his God Who did not seem to care.
The sky seemed brass to all his urgent prayers
And yet, he cried his faith with every breath,
"I know that my Redeemer liveth."

'I know that my Redeemer liveth'.
Can we, with Job, repeat these precious words?
We have our God made flesh, our living Lord,
Redeeming us from darkness, sin and loss;
Taking our place upon that cruel cross;
Presenting us before His Father's throne.
Our faith, our hope, is found in Him alone.
Can you, with Job, repeat through thick and thin,
"Though He should slay me yet I'll trust in Him.
He is my risen Lord through life, through death,
I know that my Redeemer liveth."

No Going Back

John 21

We were still unbelieving and afraid.
Jesus our Lord had risen from the grave,
We'd talked with Him, Thomas had touched His hands
And yet we doubted, did not understand
That Christ had triumphed over death and sin,
So that mankind could put their trust in Him.

Peter suggested we go back to fish.
The rest of us agreed – it was his wish.
We'd worked the boats before we met the Lord,
So now it seemed the only thing to do;
But out on Lake Tiberius that night
Our nets were empty — not a fish in sight.

The morning came, hearts sad and bodies sore
We heard a shout from someone on the shore;
"My children, have you any fish?" He called.
"Not one," we cried, not knowing Him at all.
"Throw out your nets on the right side this time."
We did – our nets were full – it was His sign.

Something about the figure on the sand:
Maybe it was the tone of His command
Made me tell Peter, " Look, it is the Lord."
In his excitement and without a word
Peter just grabbed his coat, jumped overboard
And waded to the shore to reach the Lord.

We followed after with the catch of fish,
Over a hundred more than we could wish.
Jesus had built a fire of burning coals
And had prepared a meal for hungry souls.
"Come and have breakfast," were His loving words
And by this act we knew He was the Lord.

Continued

24

'There is no going back' the Bible says,
'Forget the things behind and forge ahead.'
With Christ, who called us all to walk with Him,
And on the Cross delivered us from sin.
Submit to Him, He knows which way is best,
And in His will you will be richly blest.

Oh For a Heart

Oh for a heart, a heart like Lydia's heart,
Opened by God when Paul had done his part.
Her gift of hospitality that day
Encouraged Paul's companions on their way.
Her opened heart, her kindness and her love
Showed the reality of her trust in God.
Oh for an open heart that yearns for more —
More of the Lord — His Holy Spirit's power.

Oh for a humble heart that thinks of others,
Remembering Jesus' word "all men are brothers."
A heart to learn, as Martha slowly learned
In all her fuss and worry and concern;
Amid the pots and pans , the lowly tasks,
The unseen actions, doing what Christ asks.
Oh for a heart to serve each one we meet
And follow in Christ's steps and wash their feet.

Oh for a heart of faith and sure belief
In Christ's great love for all in pain and grief.
A woman braved a crowd to touch the Lord,
Twelve years of pain and suffering her record.
In spite of all her fears God met her need
And she received Christ's blessing on her deed.
"Go in peace, my daughter, your faith has made you
whole."
Oh for a heart of faith that trusts the Lord,
Believes His word and reaches towards His goal.

Continued

Oh for a heart like Mary's heart of love
Sitting in worship --- listening to Christ's word.
A love that sacrificed her box of nard
And poured its contents over Jesus head,
Anointing Him, her Lord, with sweet perfume
Because she knew His death was coming soon.
Oh for a heart like Mary's heart of love
Prepared to give our all to Christ the Lord.

Oh for a heart like Hannah's heart of prayer.
Within her home her life one long nightmare,
Her rival's taunts leaving her all alone.
Breaking her heart in longing for a son;
'Til God, in love and mercy answered prayer
And Samuel, her son, was born to her.
Oh for a praying heart before God's throne
That waits his answer, trusting Him alone.

Oh for a heart, a sacrifice to God,
A broken, contrite heart before the Lord,
A heart of purity, of prayer and praise
Pleasing to God Who died our souls to save.
A humble heart of yearning for our Lord
Whole hearted in obedience to His Word.
Oh for a broken heart for all in need.
Oh Lord our God for brokenness we plead.

"The sacrifices of God are a broken spirit,
a broken and contrite heart,
O God, you will not despise."
(Psalm 51:17)

Only By Grace

Grace took on flesh when Christ came to this earth,
The Saviour of men, full of grace and of truth.
Only by grace may we see God's dear Son,
Our Redeemer in glory, the victory won.

Grace opened the door of life to us all.
By Christ's death on the cross He conquered the fall.
Only by grace can the door of our heart
Be opened to those with lives falling apart.

Grace is forgiveness through Christ on the cross.
He suffered and died, became sin for us.
Only by grace has salvation been won
As God looks at our failures, He looks on His Son.

Grace justifies us through faith in our Lord.
Not by our efforts but by trust in His word.
Only by grace, not by works nor by deeds,
Does God bless us and guide us and answer our needs.

Grace is salvation for all who believe
In Jesus as Saviour and Him receive.
Only by grace can all nations be reached
By the word of the gospel faithfully preached.

Grace is our Lord; as a servant He came
Bearing our sorrows, we must do the same.
Only by grace, as He wept, can we weep
And serve, as He served, by the washing of feet.

Grace is abundant , poured out for our sin.
Where sin abounded grace flooded in.
Only by grace can we live day by day,
Hands that were wounded are guiding our way.

Continued

Grace is God's gift, free to us and all others.
"Go and tell," He commands us, "All men are brothers."
Only by grace made sufficient for us,
Can His strength, in our weakness, make perfect our trust.

Grace is God's blessing to us day by day
As we grow to be like Him and walk in His way.
Only by grace , when the Lord calls us home,
Will the journey be ended, the victory won.

Rejoice

Luke 15

While here on earth our Saviour told
About a shepherd and his fold.
He had a hundred in his flock
But one went missing from his stock.
He left the rest and went to find
The wandering one for which he yearned.
Returning with it in his arms,
"Rejoice!" he cried, "It is not harmed."

Another story Jesus told.
A woman lost a coin of gold,
Part of a precious hoard of ten.
She lit her lamp, she got her broom,
Then, diligently swept her room;
Down in a crack, behind the door,
She found her coin upon the floor;
She called her friends, "Rejoice! Rejoice!
I've found the coin which I had lost."

Again the Saviour told of one.
A father waits his erring son.
Day after day he scans the road
Until he sees the prodigal.
He runs with arms outstretched to greet,
Calls for a robe, shoes for his feet,
"Rejoice!" He cries to all around,
"Rejoice with me, the lost is found,"

The Lord delights in me, in you!
'Tis written in His word, 'tis true!
He sings a song, "Rejoice with Me,
My precious, honoured child is free."
Each one returning who was lost
Is cherished, loved, but at such cost!
The One Who died upon that tree
Rejoices over you and me!

The Apple of God's Eye

Deut. 32:10, Zechariah 2:8, Psalm 17:8

From every angle the pupil of the eye is safely guarded from attack. This is symbolic of God's protection of His own from all hostile powers that menace this precious possession. C.H.Spurgeon wrote, "You are His peculiar care, His regal treasure which he guards as 'the apple of His eye.'"

They were the 'apple of God's eye'.
Divine love chose to hear their cry
And brought them out of slavery,
Through sin and shame and suffering,
Into the land He'd promised them.
But disobedience and sin
Spoiled their relationship with Him,
Scattered them from the promised land.
Divine love still holds out His hand.
God waits, in love, for their return,
His promises are sure and firm
To Israel, He will draw nigh.
They are 'the apple of God's eye.'

Divine love gave our Lord to die.
God gave 'the apple of His eye,'
His only Son to bear the guilt
Of all our sin upon Himself.
Love to the uttermost was given,
Grace was poured out on earth from heaven.
Christ died upon that awful cross
To save us all from sin and loss.
Abundant love! Abundant grace!
Some day we'll see Him face to face
And know, in full, the reason why
We are 'the apple of God's eye.'

The Carpenter

The small boy stood in the Carpenter's shop one day,
Tears streaked the dirt on his face as he looked where 'it'
lay;
His cart, which he'd prized above all of the toys that he
had,
Lay broken and minus its wheels and the heartbroken lad,
Through his tears looked into the face of the Man standing
there.
"Can you mend my cart, please?" he asked of the kind Car-
penter.

The Carpenter smiled, placed His arm round the small boy
in tears.
At His touch the tears vanished with all of his worries and
fears.
"This is easily mended, my child, for it's one that I made
And I know how to mend broken pieces," the Carpenter
said.
"Thank you, Jesus, oh thank you," he cried, with a smile
that just grew,
"You mend broken things and I knew you would make it all
new."

Yes, our Saviour can mend broken hearts and bind up their
wounds;
Shattered homes, severed lives, become whole in the
warmth of His love.
He became One with us, and He knows how it feels when
we weep.
When we're lonely and sad and hurt feelings are buried
down deep.
For, although He was God, He was tempted and tried as we
are,
And He suffered to mend broken lives, our dear Carpenter.

The Fire

From high above the ground the child looked down,
Held in fear's grip, by awful terror bound.
Fire crackled from the walls, the roof, the doors,
Dark, choking smoke, obscured the bottom floor.
The child, held to the window in his fear,
Calling to those he could not see, just hear.

His father stood beneath his only son,
Gripped by his terror for his little one,
Seeing his child so paralysed by fear,
The crackling fire drawing so swiftly near.
The window where the boy stood looking down,
The smoke, which hid his father on the ground.

The father called out, trying to find a way
To save his boy, "My son, do as I say."
"Climb out and jump, I'll catch you in my arms,
Don't be afraid, I'll keep you from all harm."
"But Dad, the smoke is thick, I can't see through."
"Just trust me, jump my son, I can see you.

Our heavenly Father cares for you, for me,
Each step we take His loving eye can see;
Our joys and sorrows, troubles, He will share;
He longs to keep us, always, in His care.
We cannot see the way,our sight is dim,
But He can see it all, just trust in Him.

He knoweth the way that I take. Job 23:10

The Eternal God is your refuge and underneath
Are the everlasting arms. Deut. 33:27

The Miracle

Acts 3:1-10

It was hotter than usual, that afternoon,
As the sun blazed down in Jerusalem.
Crowds passed the place where I always sat
Begging for alms at the temple steps.
This was my life – disabled from birth,
This was my life – for what it was worth
Until that great day when I was reborn,
When the Saviour touched me through Peter and John.

I watched these two men, as they climbed towards me,
Hoping that they would respond to my plea.
They did not draw back or make any fuss
But said to me quietly, "Please look at us."
Expecting a gift from Peter and John
I looked into their eyes from which only love shone.
" Of silver or gold I have none," Peter said,
"But what I do have I will give you instead."

Believe me, I knew there was power all around
When he said, "In the name of Christ Jesus get up from the
ground".
He stretched out his hand, pulled me to my feet
In the midst of that crowd in that terrible heat.
Yes, my feet and my ankles grew strong as I stood,
I knew that the Name they had called on was good.
Who was He, this Jesus, of whom Peter talked?
I wanted to know by whose power I could walk.

Such joy filled my heart, my feet seemed to take wings,
And there, in that throng, I started to sing.
Praise and thanksgiving took over my song
And I danced to the temple with Peter and John.
Those servants of God told that crowd of their sin
And of how Jesus died --- they'd crucified Him.
Five thousand of them were saved by the Word,
And joined me in praising and thanking the Lord.

The Nearly Man

Mark 10:21,22

Why did I turn away from Him when I was nearly there?
Why did my courage fail me and leave me in despair
That day I knelt before Him so many years ago?
I often think about it and wish it wasn't so;
For I nearly made God's kingdom, I'll tell you ,if I can,
But nearly does not count with God and I'm the 'Nearly
Man.'

My life was very pleasant, a very rich background,
So different from the many I used to see around;
Poor beggars, always pleading, the sick, the blind, the lame,
I always gave them something - Mr. Generous - my name!
It made me feel important, made me feel good inside,
But still my heart was empty,a void I tried to hide.

I heard about this teacher, a man from Galilee,
Who was performing miracles --- so it was told to me.
My friends despised and hated Him,were jealous of His
fame,
The people flocked to see Him as He healed the sick and
lame;
The Pharisees were furious and making quite a fuss,
He had a grasp of Scripture, but no training, unlike us.

In spite of all my riches, my houses and my land,
I felt empty, life was pointless, everything seemed bland.
Jesus' preaching, Jesus' teaching, of a love much greater far
Than we heard of from our Rabbis drew me, and I didn't
care
Who was watching, criticising, as I knelt upon the ground
At the feet of the man Jesus and the people standing round.

Continued

"What must I do, I asked Him, for this life you talk about?
The commandments that you mention I've always kept since youth,
But still there's something missing, so I've come to you today
For the life you call eternal. I want to know the way."
He gazed at me, so sadly, His look pierced to my soul,
"Sell all you own," He challenged, "then follow where I go."

The years have passed too quickly,I look back with great regret;
I spend time in the temple, help the poor and those who lack;
Nothing brings a sense of peace; I missed God's Son back then.
I've wept hot tears and pleaded, my chance won't come again,
My hours and days are futile, my death is close at hand;
Say 'yes,' my friends, when God calls you, don't be a 'Nearly Man.'

Matthew 19: 16f

The idea for this poem came from Rev. Sidlow McFarland.

The Emmaus Road

Luke 24

We walked the Emmaus Road to home with heavy hearts
that day;
Our friend, our dearest Lord, was dead,
We couldn't even pray
For all our hopes and plans, our dreams were lying in the
dust,
Jesus of Nazareth was dead –
It all seemed so unjust.

We could not understand how all had happened there that
day,
And then a stranger joined us as we walked along the way.
He seemed to see our broken hearts and asked why this was
so
And we began to tell Him all;
We thought he didn't know.

We told Him how our dearest friend had been condemned
to die;
Shamed, beaten, nailed upon a cross, all we could ask was
'why?'
Why did it have to end like this?
Our thoughts went round and round,
We thought He'd save our nation. Loose the chains that
held us bound.

We also told Him how these things took place three days
ago,
And now the tomb was empty – some women found it so
When they had gone to visit it --
His body was not there, and angels told them,
"He's alive, He's risen. He's not here."

Continued

This stranger, who had walked with us
And listened as we talked, then spoke to us,
Reminding us of what the Prophets taught;
How Christ, the only Son of God, would suffer all these things
Before He entered glory, to save men from their sins.

As we approached our village, it was getting very late,
The stranger made to leave us as we stopped before our gate.
We asked Him in to stay awhile and join us for a meal,
Still ignorant of who He was – our eyes were blind – until

We sat down round the table and this stranger took the bread.
He blest it, then he broke it, and not a word was said.
As he began to share with us our eyes were opened wide.
We recognised our Saviour. He really was alive.

As we recognised our Saviour He disappeared from sight;
Back to Jerusalem we rushed although so late at night.
We shared our news, "Christ is alive," with all those gathered there
And Peter too had seen the Lord – no longer in despair.

Again, the Lord appeared to us, "Peace be to you," He said.
We really were quite startled, and very much afraid.
"Do not be troubled," were His words, "And don't doubt what you see.
Look at my wounds, my hands, my feet." We knew then, it was He.

As we spoke of what had happened our hearts with joy were thrilled.
He told us that the scriptures must, in all things, be fulfilled.
He had to suffer on that Cross, to die and rise again.
And we, His witnesses, must take the message to all men.

Too Close

A little boy, called Jamie, fell out of bed one night,
Awakened suddenly from sleep, it gave him quite a fright.
His mother heard the sound of the bump from overhead
And finding Jamie on the floor she tucked him back in bed.
"What happened to you, Jamie, you're causing such a din?"
"Sorry", he said, "I guess I stayed too close where I got in!"

Have you moved on with Jesus or still where you got in?
Still caught by the world's pleasures, its noise and constant
din?
Is your prayer life much deeper, God's word your only
guide?
Is your faith in God increasing, with Jesus by your side?
Dear friend, if you're still stuck today at the place where
you got in,
Get down on your knees and ask the Lord to move you
closer to Him.

Walking on Water

Matthew 14:22-32

Yes, it had been a miraculous day.
Jesus had fed that large crowd in a way
That had shown us so clearly His power to provide.
Now He told us, "Get into the boat and sail to the other side."
He didn't come with us. He looked very tired.
Sometime with His Father was what He desired.

The wind was quite light when we started to sail
Late in the evening; no thought of a gale
Had entered our heads 'til a strong gust of wind
Rocked the boat, waves rose high, daylight was dimmed.
Such a storm had arisen, we felt really scared.
Where was Jesus our Friend? Did He know? Did He care?

The tempest was raging. Where, where was the Lord?
Thrown about in the boat we were battered and bruised;
Then out of the dusk, when we thought we were lost,
Came a figure, it looked like a ghost,
A man, walking towards us on top of the waves!
Then we saw it was Jesus - we knew we were saved.

I could hardly believe it; my mind said it was so.
I called out to Jesus, I just had to know
"If it really is You Lord bid me walk on the sea."
And He answered, "Come, Peter, come, walk unto Me."
I stepped out of the boat, looking only at Him,
Took a few steps and then heard the strong wind!

What was I doing? I looked down at the waves
Tumbling around me! I thought I was brave,
But as soon as I saw them fear entered my soul,
I felt myself sinking, that water was cold!
"Lord, save me," I shouted, and there was His hand
Lifting and holding me up - I could stand!

Continued

40

The waves were still rough as He held on to me.
We walked to the boat, in that wild, rolling sea.
"Where is your faith, Peter, why did you doubt?"
He whispered to me as we boarded the boat.
The wind suddenly ceased, we gazed at the Lord
And recognised Him as the true Son of God.

When you pass through the waters do not be afraid,
Those rough waves will never go over your head.
The Saviour is with you, stretch out your hand,
His pierced hand will hold you and help you to stand.
Fix your eyes on the Christ, the dear Son of God,
Your faith will grow strong as you trust in His word.

What Have You Got

2 Kings 4:1-7

She came to Elisha in all her distress,
Crying her need, her life was a mess;
Her husband, a prophet, had died and left debts,
And men were demanding, ' the bills must be met.'
She hadn't the means, her position was grave.
They had threatened to take her two sons as slaves!
What was she to do? She was at her wit's end;
So she came to Elisha, her husband's close friend.

"How can I help you? What have you got?"
"Only a little oil left in the pot".
"Go to your neighbours, to all near and far,"
The prophet instructed. "Borrow their jars,
Get all you can and return to you home,
Close you door tight on yourself and your sons.
Fill each of the jars from your own little pot
And soon you will see a miracle wrought."

The widow obeyed the prophet's advice
And each jar was filled to the brim in a trice.
The oil in her pot multiplied as she poured,
Each jar was filled – there just weren't any more!
The oil in her own pot then ceased to flow.
How had it happened? She wanted to know.

The woman returned to Elisha, who said,
"Now, sell the oil, all your debt will be paid.
You and your sons can live on what's left.
God has answered your need, your sons are now safe."
The widow had used the little she'd got,
And God, in His mercy, had made it a lot.

Your Passport

Excitement had gripped the whole family,
They had planned all year for this day;
Dad, Mum and daughter and Jamie their teen-age son.
The cases stood packed in the hallway,
Last minute jobs were all done.
"Are you sure you have tickets and passports?"
Was the question on every tongue.

The airport was noisy and crowded,
The line to the check- in was long,
But excitement made it less boring
And soon they reached the queues head.
The stewardess examined the passports
Then looked closely at Jamie, the son,
"You need to have your own passport,"
Was her statement, which stunned everyone!

Bewilderment gripped the whole family;
Dad asked what the stewardess could mean?
"Your son must have his own passport
Now he's the age of sixteen."
What were they to do? The time was so short!
They moved out of the queue to give it some thought.

The solution they came to left Jamie behind!
Dad made many phone calls and soon put things right;
Grandma arrived, took Jamie home over- night,
Arrangements were made for his flight the next day.
A passport was issued for the length of his stay
And he rejoined his family without further delay.

Continued

Our God has provided the passport we need
To use on the journey of life He decreed.
Christ is our passport – His likeness the stamp
Signed by His blood , when from sin we repent.
Have you got your passport? Is Jesus your guide?
Are you travelling to heaven with Him to abide?

This poem was written for Sam Miskelly,
    The incident happened in his family!

She Praised Him

She Praised Him

Luke 13:10-17

She'd dragged her twisted body, once again,
Into the synagogue - so full of pain,
Bent double for the past, long eighteen years,
Gone beyond hope of healing, beyond tears;
Familiar faces, lost above, in light,
The ground on which she trod dark to her sight.
So, once again, she sought to find release,
Within God's house her aching soul found peace.

But, in the synagogue, that Sabbath day
A Stranger took the floor to teach and pray.
Something about His voice caught her keen ear,
Love radiated from Him, stilled her fear.
He spoke to her by name, "You are set free,
You are released from your infirmity."
She felt His touch - it seemed as if a cord
Had snapped - she stood upright - she praised the Lord.

This woman, bound by Satan eighteen years,
Condemned to pain of body, darkness, fears,
Met with the Son of God that Sabbath day,
Received release and went upon her way.
She praised the Lord for freedom from her sin,
Rejoicing now, ready to follow Him.
Are you still crippled, held by sin's strong cords?
Jesus will set you free - to praise the Lord.

Mother Love

John 6:1-13

"I won't need a lunch," said her small son that day.
"I'm not going far, just a short way away."
"But you'll get so hungry," his mother replied,
"You'll miss your good lunch, you'll be empty inside.
Just take these five loaves and these two little fish,
They're easily carried, please do as I wish."

The boy took the lunch and went down to the sea
Where Andrew, his Uncle, had said he would be.
There seemed to be thousands of people around
Most of them sitting in groups on the ground.
His Uncle was there with a number of men,
Among them he recognised Jesus, his Friend.

The small boy stood listening, He heard Jesus say
"You feed the crowd," Andrew looked in dismay
At the people all waiting. What were they to do?
The small boy pushed forward calling, "Uncle Andrew,
My lunch is small but it's better than none,
Jesus can use it to feed everyone."

We all know the story, how thousands were fed
With two little fishes and five loaves of bread.
But the gift the boy gave to be used by God's Son
Was prepared by a mother who cared, in her home.
Like Mary, who poured out her ointment, in love,
This service for Jesus was noted above.

- A poem for Mother's Day

Under His Wings

Psalm 91:4

Chalky, the mother hen, pecked warily
Round the stones of the farmyard while keeping her eye
On her brood of small chicks cheeping away
Like small children at play.
But something was troubling the white mother hen,
There was smoke in the air, swirling into her pen.
The farm dog was barking, she heard people shout,
So, calling her brood from danger without,
She settled them safely under her wings
Waiting to see what the minutes would bring.

The barn was ablaze, the flames leaping high,
The hen saw them dancing across the sky.
She settled more firmly on top of her brood
Holding her chickens as close as she could.
The flames leaped across her, her body was scorched,
But, after the fire when somebody searched,
The poor hen was dead, but there, on the ground
Still under her wings, quite safe and sound,
Her chickens were nestling, kept safe from the flames
By the love of their mother, whose life they had claimed.

In the business of living our lives day by day
We meet trials and pain as we walk in Christ's way.
Heartache and sorrow are part of our lot
For this life on earth is all that we've got.
If we don't know the Christ Who has said in His word
That in trouble His wings are outstretched like a bird's.
His children can hide when danger surrounds,
Under those wings where safety is found.
Do you know the peace Christ the Saviour can bring
To a life safely hidden under His wings?

No Condemnation

John 8:1-11

One day, to a temple, the Pharisees came
Dragging a woman - her head bowed in shame.
Approaching the Saviour they listed her sins,
Seeking an answer to use against Him.
She was guilty - a sinner - caught in the act;
Moses law stated - they quoted the fact -
That she should be stoned, put to death by the crowd.
They waited, these teachers, self-righteous and proud,
A word from the Saviour, a word they could use
Against Him, in judgment; these arrogant Jews.

The Saviour of men bent down to the ground,
Not looking at her or the people around,
While the Pharisees carried on making a fuss
He wrote, with His finger, some words in the dust.
Then, standing again He spoke in strong tones,
"He who is sinless cast the first stone."
Again he bent down and wrote in the dust
As the Pharisees, lacking all mercy and trust,
Looked at each other in shame and dismay,
Then, those self-righteous Jews, one by one, went away.

All was still in the sunshine, there wasn't a sound
As the Saviour stood up and looked all around,
"Where are those who accuse you?" the Son of God asked
As He turned to the woman and faced her, at last,
"Has no one condemned you - not one of these men?"
"Not one," she replied in confusion and shame.
With love, and compassion the Lord looked at her,
This poor, guilty woman whose burden He shared,
"Go now, sin no more," came the gentle reply,
"They cannot condemn you and neither do I."

Continued

All have sinned and come short of the glory of God,
There are no exceptions, we read in His word.
Those censorious Pharisees, bound by the law,
Who thought they were perfect, without any flaw,
The woman accused and man-handled by them.
We too, in our pride and our haste to condemn,
Point the finger at others and fail to perceive
That all are condemned unless we believe
In the Saviour Who loved us and saved us from sin.
There is no condemnation if we are "in Him."

No Strange God

Job 19: 26-27

A little girl, in India, lay dying
Amid the filth and squalor of her home.
Disease had gripped her life, now she was lying
Waiting for death - no friend to call her own.

A neighbour called a doctor from the mission
To see the child, so thin and pale and worn;
No medicine could cure the child's condition,
Or poverty, in which she had been born.

The doctor sat beside the filthy pallet
Telling the little one of Jesus' love;
How He especially cared for little children,
How He would welcome her in heaven above.

The dying child had learned to love this Jesus
Who cared enough to suffer death for her,
The doctor held her hand and drew her closer,
But still the child seemed full of fear, unsure.

"What worries you, my child?" he asked her, gently,
As wearily she gave a little moan;
"All will be strange, all strangers there in heaven,
I'l have no friends, no one to call my own."

The doctor smiled at her and held her closely,
She was so small, so sick, so full of care.
"My little one, you do not need to worry,
Jesus you know - He is your friend - He's there'"

The idea for this poem came from Edges of His Ways by
Amy Carmichael. January 17.
Deut. 32:12 "There was no strange God with Him."

Skin On

A much loved little girl was taught, by Mum,
Who loved the Lord, that she was not alone,
God who was her Friend, Who kept her in His care,
She had no need of fear for He was there,
His ear was ever listening for her call,
He even knew the smallest sparrow's fall.
The child was happy with her mother near,
Her life was full of laughter and few tears.

One evening, after all her prayers were said
And mum had tucked her safely into bed,
A dreadful storm blew up, the light'ning flashed,
The room lit up and thunder rolled and crashed.
The child was wakened by the roaring sounds,
The flashing light - her heart began to pound -
"Please come and get me quickly, Mum," she cried,
Hiding her eyes, shaking and terrified.

Her mother caught the child up in her arms
Shielding her little girl from further harm;
The little arms clung tightly round mum's neck,
Her sobs began to lessen and abate.
"Why were you so afraid with God so near
To guard, protect, and keep you safe, my dear?"
The little one relaxed, her fears all gone -
"I wanted someone near who has skin on."

Are you someone to whom your friends can turn
When trouble strikes, illness, bereavement comes?
Do you know when to listen, when to speak?
Are you the one whom all your friends will seek
When they, in doubt, in sorrow or in fear
Need someone with a sympathetic ear?
Are you as solid friend amid life's storms?
Are you God's agent here who has "Skin On?"

I do not remember where I heard this story but I think it
speaks volumes in a humorous way.

Love

A clergyman, one drab and dismal day,
Sat in his study, wond'ring what to say
To those who, faithful week by week would meet
Next sabbath day, in church, God's face to seek
And listen to to the Word that he would bring,
A Word of help, of love from Christ the King,
A Word of comfort, courage for the faint,
A Word of challenge to the needy saint.

Poor Mrs. Thomas, widowed in her teens,
Dreaming about the past - what "might have been."
Still lonely, bitter, harbouring a grudge
Against her heavenly Father, Who, in love
Had taken her Tom away from all his pain,
Blind to the fact, her loss, her husband's gain.
What could he say to help her understand
That God was near and she was in His hand?

The minister sat, head bent in humble prayer,
He sensed God's love and knew His Presence there.
But, how to bring that knowledge to his flock?
When to his ears there came a gentle knock,
And then, into the room his small son came,
His face aglow, his shoulders wet with rain.
"Why are you here, what do you want, my lad?"
"Nothing," he said, "just to be with you, Dad."

His prayer was answered by a little child
Whose love for him had brought him to his side
Unsought and undeserved. God in His grace
Had sent His Son to save a sinful race.
He'd left His Father's side and come to earth,
A little child of poor and humble birth.
Had lived and walked close to His fellow-man
And sought, in service, to fulfill God's plan.

Continued

54

His own dear son had shown to him God's love.
Wanting his presence - just as God above
Wanted, because of love, to sojourn here,
His Presence our delight, freeing from fear
The lonely one whose grief He came to bear -
The burdened one whose load He came to share -
Just to be with us - ever, always near.
Be still, my soul, and sense His Presence here.

Let Him In

Revelation 3:20

The woman's cottage stood beside the gates
Of beautiful Balmoral's vast estates,
She often saw the carriage of the Queen
Drive in and out - allowed herself to dream
That maybe, one day soon, Victoria would come
And share a 'cuppa in her humble home.

She'd shared her dreams with some whom she'd called friends,
Who'd laughed at her - not meaning to offend.
Her feelings easily hurt, she'd then attacked
Believing they were mocking at her back.
Words like sharp arrows were exchanged
And now her door was locked against her friends.

Her neighbours tried to heal the awful breach,
And, one by one, had come and tried to reach
The hand of friendship to her once again,
But all their kindly efforts were in vain.
Her door was closed to every single one,
Greatly discouraged they left her quite alone.

One quiet afternoon she heard a knock
Upon her door, as usual, fast locked.
She did not move - she would not open up -
Again, and once again the door was knocked,
"Oh, go away, leave me alone," she cried,
"My door is locked you'll never get inside."

Footsteps retreated down the garden path
And the old woman, shaking in her wrath
Against the one who'd dared to knock her door,
Pulled back the curtain - and her heart was sore -
For now she saw her visitor had been
None other than Victoria, the Queen!

Continued

One, greater than Victoria, still stands
Outside your door, knocking with pierced hand.
"Oh, hear my voice," He calls, "open your door,
My blood was shed for all, for rich and poor
That God, my Father, could forgive your sin.
Open your heart's door and let me in."

No Other Plan

"Who have you left behind to spread the story?"
The angels asked when Christ returned to glory.
"The world is very wide, what is your plan
To reach, from east to west, the souls of man?
How will they hear the news up north, down south,
So many, many miles by word of mouth?
Who have you taught and trained that they may go
Into the world to let all people know
Your blood was shed to save man from his sin,
You died on Calvary all souls to win?"

The angels waited for the Lord's reply,
Their glorious Lord returned from earth to sky.
"I've left behind eleven simple men
To preach the Word - eleven faithful friends,
Among them Peter, John and James."
"But Lord," the angels questioned him again,
"Peter denied You thrice, these are weak men,
Uneducated, tongue-tied fishermen,
For, when You needed them they ran."
The Lord replied, "I have no other plan."

"You are my witnesses," the Saviour said.
Peter was one, although weak and afraid
At Pentecost he witnessed to the crowds,
Each in his own tongue heard, both clear and loud,
That Christ, the crucified, ascended Lord
Had bidden His disciples preach the Word.
And so, because they faithfully obeyed
Two thousand years ago, we all today,
Are called to be His witnesses to man,
Faithful to Christ - Who had "no other plan."

This story as been told in many places by many men. I
think it makes a challenging poem.

The Rich Fool

Luke 12:13-21

"What will I do with this tremendous yield?"
The farmer asked, as he surveyed his fields.
As far as eye could see rich waves of grain
Stretched in their beauty, over all the plain.
"My crop is great, my barns are much too small,
So many tons of grain will crack the walls.
I will pull down my barns and bigger build.
My future's safe, my coffers are well filled,
I'll eat and drink, enjoy myself my way,
My life will now be one long holiday."

The Lord was listening to this rich man's boast,
It seemed that "I" and "my" were used the most
About his wealth, his property, his grain,
As if he, not the Lord, had sent the rain
And made the sun, the seasons, as reward
For all his labour - now he would lie back,
Enjoy it all exactly as he liked.
"You are a fool, tonight you will be dead,
Who then will have your property?" God said.

How many live today without the Lord,
Possessions, riches, holidays abroad
Their only aim, enjoyment now, today,
The future, death, a long, long way away,
No thought of Christ Who died, that they might live
The more abundant life He came to give?
He waits, in love, to save us from our sins,
His grace extends to all who come to Him.
Choose Christ Who loves you, now, oh, don't delay
Or someday soon, "Thou fool," you'll hear Him say.

Words

Proverbs 12:18

A wiseman, talking to his son one day
Became concerned, on hearing what the young man had to
say.
Gossip and boasting lightly tripped off his tongue,
Men's characters were ruined by the words of one so young.
Words of hate, not healing: words of flattery and lies
Assaulted, disappointed and appalled the one so wise,
The power of death and ruin from the careless mouth of one,
His dearest, his beloved child, his treasured only son.

The wiseman took his problem to the Lord in humble prayer
Seeking for His wisdom, how to teach his son and heir.
The Lord his prayer soon answered, an idea came to mind,
He filled a bag with feathers and in words both firm and kind
Commanded, that his son shake out the feathers in the street,
Where gentle breezes lifted them, like husks of winnowed
wheat
O'er roof tops, chimneys, trees, they sailed, down alleyways,
Through gates through open windows, over fields, in thorny
hedges caught.

The boy returned and told his father all that had been done,
But stared in blank amazement when the wiseman asked his
son
To take the bag and fill it with the feathers once again.
"Impossible," the young man said, "my task would be in
vain.
Each feather's gone beyond recall, I cannot get them back,
They're lodged in many places, cellar steps and chimney
stacks."
"Gone like your words," the man replied, "your careless, hurt-
ful words,
Lodged in the broken hearts of men pierced by your words,
like swords."

This poem came from an illustration given in a sermon by
Rev. Roy Magee.

The Lord's Supply

1 Kings 17

The drought was extreme in the midst of the land
But Elijah was fed by God's generous hand.
The brook had dried up, the ravens had gone,
The bread, the meat and the water were done.
The word of the Lord reached the Prophet's ears,
Renewing his faith and allaying his fears.
"Go at once into Sidon, a widow is there,
She'll continue to feed you, her food you will share."

Elijah obeyed the command of the Lord,
The widow was there - God had given His word.
She was gathering sticks to make, what she feared,
Would be a last meal, when Elijah appeared.
"Would you bring me a drink?" God's Prophet then said,
"And please, I am hungry, a small piece of bread."
"As God is my witness, all I have got
Is a handful of flour and some oil in a pot."

The widow explained she was going back home
To make a last meal for herself and her son.
Her larder was bare, she did not deny,
When this food was done they expected to die.
Elijah spoke gently, "Please don't be afraid,
The Lord God of Israel has come to your aid.
First make me a meal, a small cake of bread,
Then a meal for yourself and your son, as you said.
The oil in the pot and the flour in the bin
Will not fail 'till the day when the Lord sends the rain."

Continued

The widow believed what the Prophet had said;
She returned to her home, made her loaf of bread,
She gave to Elijah, she ate with her son,
The flour did not fail, the oil didn't run done.
God had promised Elijah He'd supply all his needs,
The widow believed put her faith into deeds,
And for all of the years when the rain did not fall,
There was plenty to eat, enough for them all.

In the middle of drought with no promise of rain
Our God fed His servant with water and grain.
He kept to His word - His supply would not fail -
The birds did His bidding - the widow as well.
Do we believe God Who has said, in His word
He'll supply all your needs from His generous store?
His grace overflowing through Jesus, His Son,
Is ours when we ask Him, in prayer, at His throne.

His Tools

He left the glory of His Father's throne,
Born of a virgin to a carpenter's home,
Played as a child among wood shavings dropped
From the timber hewed in Joseph's shop;
Grew into manhood learning all the skills,
The use of a plane and hammer, nails and drill
To fashion wood, the commonplace He made,
The plough, the yoke, a cradle for a babe.
Jesus, the Son of God, served rich and poor,
And all were blessed who entered at His door.

The soldiers took the tools of Jesus trade
And with them formed a cross, on which they spread
The Son of God - timber, rough hewn, was used
To make His cross - nails pierced and bruised
Those gentle hands and feet - driven through flesh and
bone -
While He hung there suffering, alone -
By men who took the fine tools of His trade
And without mercy hammered in those nails.
Sin, not the nails and hammers caused the death
Of Jesus - Carpenter - of Nazareth.

In His Hand

Isaiah 48:10

Jeremiah 18:6

It was simply a bar of iron as it lay on the blacksmith's
bench,
Heavy and plain and useless, worth only a handful of pence.
But the blacksmith took it and worked it; through fire and
water it went,
It was hammered and heated and shaped and cooled,
When the blacksmith had finished he laid down his tools
And, shining like silver, there lay on the bench
Four useful horseshoes worth some hundreds of pence.

It was simply a bar of iron as it lay on the factory floor,
Heavy, plain and useless, worth a few pounds, not more.
But a skilled man took it and formed it,
It was shattered and broken in bits,
Then through many machines those bits were fed.
They were sharpened and shaped and polished and made
Into needles so fine and so smoothly ground
That they sold in the shops for some hundreds of pounds.

It was simply a bar of iron as it lay in the jeweller's hand,
Heavy and plain and useless, worth nothing, except to this
man,
For he ground it and filled it and shaped it
'Till it seemed that nothing was left,
But that bar was transformed by the artist's hand,
From plain, heavy iron appeared a watch,
Delicate, fine, and so perfectly formed
That it sold in the shops for thousands of pounds.

Continued

Do you ever feel useless and pressured and down
And trouble lasts day after day?
Do God's dealings seem endless and troubles endure
No matter how often you pray?
But, just like the bar in the craftman's hand,
Beaten and hammered and polished and carved,
Those who suffer through trials yield most to the Lord
And bring blessing to others and glory to God.

This poem is dedicated to my sister, Peggy, who has shown
much love and patience in recent days.

Silence

Matthew 15:23
"He answered her not a word."

Silence - only silence was the answer
That greeted all my pleadings, tears and prayers.
It seemed the sky was brass, God did not hear,
And yet, I knew that Christ my Lord was near.
In tears I cried, "What does this silence mean?"
And then, one night, God answered in a dream.

He showed three women bowed in silent prayer,
And o'er the first He bent, whisp'ring to her
In tender tones, sweet words of love
And smiled and touched her gently from above,
Then stood beside the second woman there
But only placed His hand upon her hair!

Then, in my dream, as silently I watched,
He passed the third abruptly, not one touch
Or tender word of gentle look was sent
Towards the woman there in worship bent.
I thought, "She must have deeply grieved the Lord
Not to receive, at least, one look or word."

Troubled by what I'd seen and by my thoughts,
The Lord Himself stood by me as I fought
To understand the meaning of my dream;
How to interpret all that I had seen.
"Oh woman, how you have misjudged my loving care,
Listen and learn all I'm about to share."

"The first is weak in faith, needs every day
To have my voice, my hand, guiding her way.
The second woman, kneeling now in prayer
Is stronger in her faith, her love, deeper,
And I am training her to trust my word
And grow in selfless service to her Lord."

Continued

66

The third, in prayer, trusts Me so utterly
That words from Me, are quite unnecessary.
She's not dismayed by circumstance, she knows,
'Tho reason, sense and instinct all oppose,
That pain and suffering now, not understood,
Will, one day, work together for her good."

I wakened from my dream, my heart at peace,
My tears, my prayers, my pleadings all had ceased.
His silent gift was strength within my soul,
Complete and utter trust from me His goal.
So,though I do not understand His ways,
I'll trust His word, "I'm with you all the days."

The idea for this poem came from Streams in the Desert by
Mrs. Cowman.

The Challenge

Proverbs 24:10

"If you falter in times of trouble how small is your strength"

This word of challenge came when, I, at length,
Steeped in pity, sought, in prayer, the Lord
And asked from Him some comfort from His word,
Some hope, some promise in my hour of need.
But, what was this? Not words of help; indeed
Words of rebuke - reproach - had reached my ears,
Sending their challenge to my self pitying tears,
Making me look inside myself to see
My lack of faith in Christ Who died for me.

Pain in my body, sharper pain of heart
Had conquered courage, setting me apart -
Looking within - not upwards to my Lord;
Listening instead to friends whose well meant words
Caused me to think my burdens heavier,
My trials greater far than I should bear.
And so, self pity swamped each day and hour
Grieving the Spirit, limiting His power,
Until God's word challenged my unbelief,
Strengthening my inmost soul, restored my faith.

This poem was written a few years ago when I was waiting
for a scan and when my private heartbreaks almost overwhelmed me.

For Me

You left your Father's home above, Jesus, for me,
Came to this earth, His best beloved, Jesus, for me.
You took my form, my weaker frame, Jesus, for me,
A humble servant, You became, Jesus, for me.

You trod this earth, lived among men, Jesus, for me,
That one day with You I may reign, Jesus, for me,
You healed the sick, the hungry fed, Jesus, for me,
That I might know Your power to save, Jesus, for me.

You taught Your friends Your gracious words, Jesus, for me,
That I might prove Your promises, Jesus, for me,
You suffered torture, pain and shame, Jesus, for me,
And dragged Your cross to Calvary, Jesus, for me.

You bore your Father's hidden face, Jesus, for me,
And hung upon a wooden cross, Jesus, for me,
You took my sin, You bled and died, Jesus, for me,
And You, God's Son, were crucified, Jesus, for me.

By God's great power You rose again, Jesus, for me,
And intercede at His right hand, Jesus, for me,
A home in heaven You've prepared, Jesus, for me,
And all eternity You'll share. Jesus, for me.

Service

John 13:1-17

Jesus - You wrapped a towel round your waist,
You knelt before them there and washed their feet
Amid their weak protests, their drawing back,
You, Saviour, Son of God, by this one act
Became their servant - showed the sons of men
That they should do as You had done to them.

Lord, I am tired, my burden much too great,
Up early morning, not in bed 'till late,
Cleaning and ironing, cooking, washing up
Mountains of dishes, saucepans, mugs and cups.
Day after day the same jobs one by one.
"I washed your feet, you do as I have done."

Lord - I am tired - so many loud demands,
No moments for myself, I need six hands.
Expected to be there to dry up tears,
Listen to young, to old, their joys and fears.
Lord, I am tired, I feel so much alone!
"I washed your feet, you do as I have done."

So I have heard Him whisper day by day
When, full of self pity I have lost the way.
He's tried to teach me from His precious word
"The servant is not greater than His Lord."
Each task performed is service to God's Son.
"I washed your feet, you do as I have done."

This poem was the outcome of a period of caring for the
family. I had been studying John 13 prior to this time and
Jesus clearly recalled His Word to me one "crisis" day when
I was being sorry for myself.

A Child's Lament

"I want my daddy back," this poignant cry
Rang from a little girl as she stood by
An open grave in wind and rain.
A week ago they'd played in sunny Spain,
And now, her daddy, whom she'd dearly loved
Was dead - had gone away to heaven above.
Her mum was crying as she clutched her hand,
The child, just eight; she did not understand
Why evil men had come that dreadful night
And used their guns to kill all those in sight.
She did not know her dad would not be home,
"I want my daddy back," she softly moaned.

We do not understand the reasons why
Men hate their fellow men, why men die,
Except that God has given all men free will,
And some, consumed with hate, set out to kill,
To maim and to destroy those they believe
Threaten their way of life; they can't concieve,
Perhaps they do not know, God's clear command
"Thou shalt not kill," or want to understand!
And all across our land the question, "Why?"
Why does our God allow good men to die?
Why does He not do something - intervene -?
But God does understand the pain, the loss.
His Son was nailed upon a wooden cross
By evil men consumed by hate for Him.
God watched His only Son dying, pain wrecked.
He understands, "I want my daddy back."

This poem is dedicated to all who have lost loved ones in
the "troubles."

She Touched Him

She Touched Him

Mark 5:25-34, Luke 8:43-48

Many women, over the years, must have wondered about
this woman who touched the hem of Christ's garment and
what her life was like during those years of suffering. I tried
to think myself into her situation as I wrote these words.
May all of you who read them find that her story is as rel-
evant today as it was all those years ago.

Twelve long years she'd suffered
Loneliness and shame,
All her money gone now,
Nothing left but pain.
"Sorry I can't help you,"
Each doctor shook his head,
It seemed that life was finished
She must end her days in bed.

Many neighbours gathered round
When first she'd taken ill,
Cooking, cleaning,
Offers more than she could fill;
But the pain had changed her temper
And her tongue had grown sharp,
Disappointment made her bitter,
The future looked so dark.

Former friends "forgot" to call now,
"Thankless task,"she'd heard them say.
She'd forgotten God now
He just seemed too far away.
Too far distant to be caring
For a woman racked with pain,
Far too busy to be bothered,
He wouldn't even know her name.

Continued

So the days passed, all too slowly,
And twelve years had come and gone,
No hope left now, none to help her,
She was saddened and forlorn.
But help was round the corner,
It is true what people say,
That "when you reach your tether's end
God meets you in the way."

She heard the sound of knocking,
Was that someone at the door?
Painfully she struggled
From her pallet on the floor.
"Have you heard about this Jesus
The Man from Galilee?
He can heal all our diseases,
He can still a raging sea."

"Why don't you seek Him out now?"
Said her neighbour at the door,
"He's coming through our village,"
"But the crowd will throng Him sore,
How will I ever reach Him
How make Him hear my call?
If I can only touch Him,
It won't matter if I fall."

"Oh, please, don't push so roughly,
Please, let me through the crowd,
I must get near the Master,
I've no strength to cry aloud,
One more step and I can reach Him
One more step - I see the hem
There, I've touched Him, oh the freedom,
Oh, the freedom from the pain."

Continued

"Someone touched me," said the Master,
"Someone has been healed today,"
The disciples in amazement pointed
To the crowd along the way.
"Many, Lord, have touched you,
The people throng around."
But the Lord was softly speaking,
A woman kneeling on the ground.

"Go in peace, my daughter,
Your faith has made you whole."
She found healing for her body
And joy for her soul.
The future bright before her
She used her hours to tell
Of the day she touched the Master,
The day He made her well.

Many years have passed since Jesus
Healed this woman of her pain,
But the message through the ages
Hasn't changed, it's just the same.
You need healing, you need freedom,
You must forget your pride,
Just reach out and touch the Saviour,
Push your way right to His side.

Martha's Story

Luke 10:38-42

Many women, like myself, have been able to identify with
Martha when they have found themselves in a similar situation in the kitchen, while someone else, who could be helping, seems to be sitting at ease. Our Lord showed Martha
what her priorities should be. May this poem help readers
to recognize the "one thing more needful" and to choose
"that good part which shall not be taken away."

It was hot, that summer morning
In the town of Bethany,
When my brother came to tell me
That the Master had been sighted
Down the road, not far away.
"Martha, Martha," Lazareth called me,
"Do you hear me when I say
He'll be here in time for dinner,
He will eat with us today."

Yes, I head him call that morning,
And I'm ashamed to say
That I didn't answer civilly
To his summons right away.
It was hot, you see, and Mary
She was out, I don't know where,
She was always helping others
It just seemed she didn't care
That the cooking and the cleaning
And the washing all was there
To be done, by good old Martha,
I was always there.

Continued

Well - on that eventful morning
I just had to start myself
To the cooking and the cleaning,
There'd be twelve and then
The Master, Lazarus, Mary and myself.
What to give them, where to seat them?
Place clean towels on the shelf,
Leave fresh water by the doorway,
They'd be tired, they'd need to rest.
Where is Mary, is she coming?
Lazarus, call her, is she deaf?

Soon I heard the shouts of children,
They had heard the tramp of feet,
Is that kettle boiling, Mary
Have we prepared enough to eat?
By my sister too was running
With the children, there to greet
The disciples and the Master
As they turned into our street.

I confess it, I was angry
Why should I have to stay?
I was Martha, good old Martha
Always there - I'd heard them say
"You can count on good old Martha
She'll feed them all today."

Through the window I could see them
Coming up the dusty road,
And my heart was sore within me
As I pondered on my load.
"The meal is nearly ready,"
I could hear my brother say
As I placed the bread and fishes
On the plates upon the tray.

Continued

Where is Mary, can't she help now?
There she sits upon the floor
Listening to the Master's teaching,
I can hear them through the door.
"Master, I need help now,
Send my sister to my aid,
All sit down around the table."
(One would think I was the maid).

Then the Master turned towards me
As I frowned and fussed about,
And His voice came softly calling
Calming all my fears and doubts.
"Martha, Martha, leave your dishes
Leave the pots upon the fire,
Join your sister, sit down here now
We will eat it by and by.
You have worked so hard, dear Martha
We will not forget your deeds,
But your sister Mary's wiser
She's aware of others needs,
You must feed the Spirit also,
It takes time and prayer to know
All the Good our God has given,
All the love He has to show."

Many joys and many sorrows
The Master shared with us.
Lazarus, our brother, died here
And the Master raised him up.
Well I do remember standing
By that grave upon the hill,
And the words He spoke in comfort
Are vivid to me still;
"I am the resurrection and the life,"
He said that day.
And He proved it to me later
By His death at Calvary.

The Three Trees

I first heard the story "The Three Trees" at a morning assembly in Euston Street Primary School. It was told by a Presbyterian minister who gave it the following interpretation. Many young people dream of the future and of the form they would like it to take. These dreams do not often come true but, with the Lord as their guide, they may be sure that their future will be far more wonderful than any dream. I was very impressed by the story and make it into this poem.

Tall and stately the three trees stood
Close together, deep in the wood.
Years it had taken to make them grow,
Sun and wind and rain and snow;
Now they were ready, these beautiful trees,
Dreaming together of what they would be.

"I know what I'll be," said the first tall tree,
"When the woodman uses his axe on me.
I'll be a cradle, carved and rare
To rock to sleep a baby fair,
A cradle fit for a royal house,
A beautiful cradle will be my choice."

"What will I be?" murmured the second tree,
"I love the winds that blow over the sea;
A graceful ship with tall white sails,
And a cargo of spices and silks in bales;
Facing the storms, sailing the seas,
A beautiful ship, that's what I'll be."

The third tree, tallest one of the three,
Looked over the forest to where he could see
Far in the distance, streets and roads,
People on foot, carts carrying loads;
"A signpost I'll be to point the way,
A beautiful signpost, for that I'll pray."

Continued

The woodman came and the three trees fell,
And what they became is the story I'll tell;
They had dreamed of their future, what they wanted to be,
A beautiful cradle, a graceful ship, a signpost clear for men to see.
They were cut, they were carved, they were hammered and nailed,
But what they became? Seemed their dreams had failed.

For the fist tall tree was a manger stall
In a stable in Bethlehem town so small;
It was filled with straw for the cattle to feed,
But once it fulfilled another's need,
And three wise men their gifts did bring
To the manger which cradled a baby King.

The second tree's future was spent on the sea,
As a strong fishing boat on Lake Galilee;
Owned by Peter and James and John
Who used it to fish in the early dawn.
And from it, a man called Jesus preached
To a crowd of five thousand upon a beach.

The third tall tree was roughly hewn,
And dragged to a hill at Jerusalem
By a Man who was wearing a crown of thorns;
This was the purpose for which He was born.
And the tree was the cross, which pointed the way,
A signpost to all of Christ's victory.

Who Is My Neighbour or The Other Sort

Many sermons have been preached on the parable of "The Good Samaritan." When I attempted to make it a poem I failed, it simply would not "come" so I gave up. Then one morning, on Radio Ulster's "Thought for the Day" I heard a Queen's University lecturer re-tell the parable, giving the "troubles" in our province as background. He set the story in Belfast, where Jesus was answering a young lawyer who had asked the question, "Who is my neighbour?"
As I listened I felt that this interpretation was the one God wanted me to use for this poem and each word and line came easily. When reciting this poem abroad I had to explain the phrase "the other sort" as it is only understood by people in Northern Ireland.

He left his home in North Belfast that day
To drive to Antrim by the motorway,
Plenty of time he had to reach the place
Appointed by his friend, and so his pace
Was moderate, forty miles an hour, quite slow;
And that was why he saw the men with hands upraised.
A car in trouble, could he give a tow?
He stopped, no thought of danger in his mind,
In his experience men were always kind.
Out of his car he stepped, and saw, too late,
Guns in their hands, their faces filled with hate.

He wakened up to waves of dark and pain
And dragged himself close to the motor lane
And there he lay, battered and bruised, clothes torn,
Waiting for help, wishing he'd not been born.
A car slowed down, and in it he could see
A figure, darkly dressed, white collar round his neck,
A cleric on his way to speak at a committee about peace.
"Help me, oh help," he raised his arm and cried,
The car drove on along the other side.

Continued

The morning passed, the sun moved overhead,
And still he lay, "Lord help me please," he prayed.
Another car slowed down beside the way,
"Help me, oh help me please, I'll gladly pay!"
The driver of the car looked all around,
And then approached the man upon the ground.
A politician he, versed in the law,
A clever man. He shuddered when he saw
The blood and bruises of the one in need.
"Best not to get involved by word or deed!'
He told himself; and off he went
To speak that night to his constituents.

The man lay still, despair had filled his mind,
Would no one help, would no one stop to find him lying
there?
Was that another car? "Please stop, please stop,"
He silently beseeched;
And then, tyres screeched, a car door slammed,
He heard the crunch of feet;
His head was raised, cool water poured between his teeth,
His cuts were gently wiped by loving hands,
Strong arms lifted him up and helped him stand
And placed him in the car.
He found himself in bed within the hour
Between cool sheets and by his side a nurse.

"Who was it brought me here?" he asked.
"Who was the man who risked his life and gave his time
To see I did not die?"
"One of the other sort," was her reply.
Our Lord, this story told, when a young lawyer, making bold
Asked Him, "Who is my neighbour, Lord?"
I've brought it up to date.
Here in this land perhaps it's not too late
To ask ourselves this question once again,
"Who is my neighbout?"
Each man who has no home, no job, who is in pain, in
need,
The "other sort," or neighbour,
Christ said, "Help him in word and deed."

The Feeding of the Crowd

John 6:1-14

Have you ever thought about that small boy who gave his lunch to Jesus? He must have been as hungry as any boy today who has spent a day by the sea but he gave all he had to the Saviour.
I pray that the boys and girls who read this poem will give their lives to the Lord.

My mother packed a lunch for me that day
I took my rod and tackle to the bay,
Five loaves and two small fishes in a cloth,
I was a hungry boy, I liked them both.
I climbed a hill and from it I could see
The clear blue waters of Lake Galilee.
The morning sun was warm, I cast my line,
It seemed to me that all the world was mine.
Upon the lake some vessels were afloat,
Among them was my Uncle Peter's boat,
And as I watched, he sailed it to the edge
Right underneath my seat upon a ledge.
And then, around the hill there came a crowd
Of men and women, calling out aloud,
"There's Peter's boat drawn upon the shore."
And as I watched, the crowd was swelled by more
Both young and old, sick, blind and lame
Streamed up the road, and up the hill they came,
All pointing to a figure on the beach
'Twas Jesus, they had come to hear him preach.
All through the morning, afternoon, all day
Those people listened, would not go away,
The sick were healed, the blind were made to see,
The lame man walked, the bound in mind set free.
The sun began to sink behind the hill,
Jesus looked tired and worn, but still

Continued

The people listened, would not go away,
"Lord, send them to the shops to buy some food,
They'll faint beside the way."
I heard my Uncles, James and Peter say.
But Jesus, in compassion, looked around,
"Bid all the people sit upon the ground
And you give them to eat," He said,
"But Lord, we have no meat or bread."
I heard the Master's words from where I sat.
My lunch forgotten, lay beside my net,
I ran to Uncle Andrew and I said,
"Here are two fish and five small loaves of bread."
Then Jesus placed His hands upon my lunch
And lifting up His eyes to heaven He prayed,
"My Father, take this offering from this lad,
We thank You for this food, 'tis all he had,
Oh, magnify it, Father, by your power
That we may feed the crowd this very hour."
Then Peter, Andrew, James and all the rest
Took from the Lord the food that He had blessed,
And all the people seated on the ground
Received it from their hands and passed it round,
Five thousand people ate more than enough,
Twelve baskets, full of scraps, were gathered up.
The Master touched me gently on the head,
"You gave Me all you had, today." He said.
"If people everywhere, would give their all to Me
Their hearts and wills and lives, they'd see
My Father multiply the seed and pour His blessing
On a world in need."

I'm old now, many years have passed
But I have vivid memories that last
Of that one day, when, as a little boy
I met the Master, and He filled my heart with joy.

Living Water

John 4:1-46

This woman's story is familiar to us all. She must have been very lonely. F.B. Meyer writes of her, "One morning, when the land was carpeted with flowers of spring, a woman awoke in the little town of Sychar that lay in the lap of twin mountains, Ebal and Gerizim. She little realised that that day would revolutionise, not her life only, but that of untold thousands.
Throughout its happenings her story would be embalmed in the history of the race, and she would take the first step which, as tradition says, ended in martyrdom."
I hope that her story will "live" for you in these words.

I had gone to the well, as I did every day
At noon all alone, 'twas the only way
To avoid the townswomen, their gossip and strife,
For the women of Sychar disapproved of my life;
They shunned any contact, I was left on my own,
So most of my time I spent in my home,

That day at the well I was happy to see
A stranger was there, He'd arrived before me.
He looked weary and tired when He'd asked for a drink,
And He was a Jew - well, it made me think:
It just wasn't done, Jews just didn't speak
To Samaritan women, and right there in the street!

He must have known, from the look on my face,
That I knew He belonged to the Jewish race.
But He spake to me of God and His gift
Of "living water," but His meaning I missed
For the well was deep, and He hadn't a rope,
Was He greater than Jacob, could He give me hope?

Continued

His words sounded strange as I listened to them,
He told me I'd never be thirsty again
If I drank of the "water" He was offering me,
I'd be saved from my sin, I'd find I was free.
And then, He just seemed to look into my life
Said, I'd had five husbands that I wasn't a wife.

Well, I thought He must be a prophet at least,
And I argued a bit about worship and such;
I spoke of Messiah, the One called the Christ
Who was promised to make all truth plain unto us,
He turned to me gently and clear as could be
Said, "I Who am speaking to you am He."

I set down my pitcher right there by the well
And ran through the town my story to tell,
"Come with me my friends, come with me and see
The man called the Christ, Who knows all about me,
I have found "Living Water," my life has been cleansed,
"Come with me my friends, and see for yourselves."

The people of Sychar all flocked to the well
And proved there the truth of the story I tell,
They met the Messiah, believed on His name,
Their sins were forgiven, their whole lives were changed.
May you, who have heard my story retold,
Drink deep of the "Water of Life," Christ the Lord.

Naomi

Ruth 1 & 2:1-3

I have always thought that the story of Ruth and Naomi
is the most beautiful love story in the Old Testament. The
words in the Authorised Version are so lovely that I have
them printed here for you to read before the poem.
And Ruth said, Intreat me not to leave thee, or to return
from following after thee: for where thou goest, I will go;
and where thou lodgest, I will lodge; thy people shall be my
people, and thy God my God:
Where thou diest, will I die, and there will I be buried: the
Lord do so to me, and more also, if ought but death part
thee and me.

My daughter Ruth will wed Boaz tomorrow,
To me it seems to be a dream come true.
Tonight, my thoughts return to days of sorrow
And days of joy, although they've been so few.

We had to leave our home and go to Moab,
Elimelech, my husband, and our sons;
My husband died, the boys wed Ruth and Orpah,
And then, they died, I thought my life was done.

Far down the years my thoughts take wing and wonder
At all God's love shown to the human race,
I thought my heart was almost torn asunder,
But God has shown me His amazing grace.

From Judah came the news - the famine's over,
Orpah and Ruth went with me on the road,
I loved them both, these girls who were my daughters,
I'd miss them when I left the land of Moab.

We kissed each other, eyes with tears o'erflowing,
Orpah returned to Moab, 'twas her home,
But Ruth clung close, with words so warm and loving
I'll keep them in my heart for years to come.

"Naomi, Mother, beg me not to leave you,
I can't go back and you go on alone,
I must go with you to the land of Judah,
Your people I will take to be my own."

"I'll live with you, Naomi, as your daughter,
And through the years your family I'll become,
I'll try to fill your loneliness with laughter,
Together we will make a happy home."

"The God you love I'll take to be my Saviour,
He's been your guide through all the passing years,
He'll keep us both in living, or in dying,
And each day we will prove His presence near."

Both old and young, we made our home together,
She gleaned the fields, and ground the corn to flour.
I praise the God of Israel Who gave her
To be my daughter in my lovely hours.

He's led us gently through our years of trial,
God of the past, the present, the future too.
And now, my Ruth will wed Boaz tomorrow,
God's love is sure, His promised word is true.

John's Story

John 21:1-14

This poem was written during a holiday in Cornwall and was inspired by a talk given by a Baptist pastor from Jersey. He spoke of the concern for the disciples' physical well being shown by the resurrected Saviour, Who had breakfast prepared for the bewildered men and served it to them Himself. Jesus is the same, yesterday, today and forever.

We were alone, Peter and James and I,
On Calvary, we'd seen the Saviour die,
He'd called us from our work to be His friends
And told us He would make us fish for men.

We thought He'd make His kingdom on this earth,
That we, His friends, would see and share its birth;
We did not understand His words so true
"The kingdom of my Father is in you."

Not knowing what to do we took our boats
And back upon the lake set them afloat,
We cast our nets and toiled all night in vain,
Our hearts were heavy, full of grief and pain.

What could we do? We did not have a choice;
Then through the mists of dawn we heard a voice
Calling us, so clear across the sea,
We did not know, at first, that it was He.

"My children, cast your nets, again on the right side,"
We looked at one another, then we tried,
And lo, behold, our nets were full of fish,
More than the best of fishermen could wish.

Then something in me seemed to strike a chord,
I said to Peter, "Look, it is the Lord."
And he, poor man, pulled on his fisher's coat
And jumped into the lake from off the boat.

Continued

We dragged the nets to land, and there,
Burned on the beach, a fire prepared
By Christ Himself, and on it fish and bread.
"Come dine with me, my friends, come dine," He said.

Our Lord, by all that happened on that morn,
Taught us a lesson in the early dawn,
That we, without His help, can nothing do,
But we, with Him, can make men's hearts anew.

Peter

This dungeon floor is cold and damp and hard,
The light is dim, the windows strongly barred,
My arms and legs are wearied by these chains,
My body bruised and broken, full of pain,
But in my heart my Saviour speaks to me
His words of comfort, "Peter, you'll soon be free."

That day, by Galilee, when Andrew said,
"Come with me Peter, come with me and see
The man called Jesus, He who is the Christ,
The true Messiah, promised from the first,"
I met my Saviour and soon now I know
He'll be the same as He was, long ago.

He called me from my boat and from the sea,
"I'll make you fish for men, come follow me."
He said, "You are the rock on which I'll build my church."
I did not know I'd leave Him in the lurch!
We followed Him in every path He trod,
And by His life we knew the Son of God.

I watched Him heal the sick and blind and lame,
He raised the dead, made straight limbs that were maimed,
He touched the leper, fed the multitude,
Five thousand at one time, He gave them food.
I saw Him tired and weary, saw Him pray,
And God His Father heard the words He'd say.

That awful day in dark Gethsemane
We heard Him pray, in deepest agony.
"Not My will Father, not My will but Thine."
I wanted to be with Him, keep Him mine,
I'd boasted once I'd never Him forsake,
And yet, I could not even keep awake!

Continued

In Pilate's hall I stood and warmed my hands,
The maid accused me, "You are of His band."
"I know Him not," I said, not once, but thrice.
Christ looked on me, and then the cock crowed twice.
I went out into the night and wept
And while He died, I reached my boat, and slept.

We met Him on the beach when He arose,
He spoke to me with gentle words of love,
"Peter, go feed my lambs, go feed my sheep,
I'll never leave you, in my hand I'll keep you."
And now, I'm here in jail, my death is due,
But through it all I've proved His promise true.

Prayer

Luke 11:1-4, Matthew 6:9-13

When thinking of a poem on prayer I felt that, as our Lord
had given us a framework which we call the Lord's Prayer, I
should build on it. Perhaps these words will help to widen
your thoughts when you pray.

"Lord, teach us to pray,"
A disciple asked of Christ the Lord, one day.
He'd seen his Master go away alone
To mountain, garden, beach or quiet home,
And there converse with God in heaven above,
One with His Father, a fellowship of love.

"Our Father God in heaven, glory to You,"
Jesus began the lesson taught to the few.
For God the Lord, Maker of earth and sea
Is loving Father, caring for you and me,
And Jesus lived His life with this one aim
That He and we might glorify God's name.

"In heaven, so on earth Thy will be done."
To do God's will Christ lived as God's own Son,
And in the garden called Gethsemane
He cried and prayed in deepest agony,
"Not My will Father, not My will but Thine,"
Then died for sin, that sin was yours and mine.

"Give us this day our daily bread."
Across the world there're many needing fed,
Our Saviour taught that loving fathers give
Not stones, but bread to sons who ask in love,
"O God our Father give us bread today,
And for our souls the Bread of Life, we pray."

Continued

Forgive our sins as we forgive all others
Who do us wrong. Christ said, "All men are brothers."
But we in sin, forgive but don't forget,
We make excuses, call it pride, and yet
Our Saviour died that we might be forgiven,
We must forgive as Christ our Lord in heaven.

"Our Father, lead us not into temptation."
We need your grace each day to carry on,
Our Saviour Christ was tempted, tried as we are
And we may triumph through the Spirit's power.
Each minute, hour and day, we know our need,
Keep us, O God from evil thought and deed.

All power belongs to You, all praise and glory,
O give us tongues to sing the wondrous story
Use hands and feet to work and walk for Thee,
Our wills we offer, ever yours to be,
O give us hearts to praise Thy holy name.
Thou Who art God the Lord, the great I Am.

The Beggar and the King

Luke 6:38

One day, a beggar, sitting in the street,
Ragged and dirty, watching hurrying feet,
Hearing the news, "the King is passing by."
Thought to himself, "Why should I have to lie
Here in the dust and dirt, hungry and cold?
The King is coming. I'll ask him for gold."

He filled his pocket with some grains of rice;
All that he had, expensive at the price.
Then pushing through the crowd he found a seat
Where he could see the King ride down the street.
The King had gold, much gold, plenty to spare,
He planned to beg, the King to give him share.

The beggar heard the crowd begin to cheer
And down the street he saw the troops appear.
The King was riding on a snow white horse,
The crowd was thick, it seemed he'd have to force
A way amongst the people gathered near,
The King was riding fast, was almost here.

The crowed fell silent as the King appeared;
He stopped his horse, a space around him cleared.
He called the beggar man from where he stood,
"O beggarman, I'm hungry, share your food."
The beggar, disappointed, in a thrice
Pulled from his pocket two small grains of rice.

The King rode on, the people disappeared,
The beggar, left alone with all his fears,
Reached into his coat, and in dismay
Saw in his hand two golden pennies lay.
Two grains of rice he'd given grudgingly
Two golden coins were given back to him.

Continued

The beggar sat amid the dirt and dust
Reviewing what had happened from the first.
The King had chosen him from all the crowd
To ask for rice, it should have made him proud.
"If I'd given the King all that I had
I'd now have gold to spare and I'd be glad."

We have a King Whose riches are untold,
He owns the earth, its diamonds and its gold.
But far more precious things He gave to us.
His life, His blood was shed upon the cross,
"Come unto Me, ye weary," hear His call,
Give Him your love, your life, your will, your all.

The Prodigal Son

Luke 15:11-24

This parable, like that of the Good Samaritan, lends itself to modern day interpretation. Many, young and old, want to "live it up" but find that there is no lasting satisfaction in the pleasures money can buy. Real joy and peace can only be found by trusting our lives to God, our Heavenly Father.

Unshaven, ragged, hungry, unable to think
"What am I doing here the worse for drink,
Searching the bins along the empty streets
For scraps of food thrown out for pigs to eat,
While back at home there's food enough to spare,
I'll ask my father for a servant's share."

The young man rose from off the cold park bench,
His clothes were dirty, torn, he looked unkempt.
A filthy hat upon his uncombed hair,
The smell of drink tainted the frosty air,
His steps unsteady, trying to stand erect,
The thought persisted, "Why don't I just go back."

His memories took him back across the years,
In youth, impatient of his father's fears,
He felt too sheltered in his happy home,
His brother older, he, the younger son;
"Give me the money now, which is my due,
I want to see the world, enjoy life too."

He roamed the world, he travelled near and far,
Always the owner of the fastest cars.
No lack of company to help him spend,
His money went on gambling, drink and friends.
He never thought to send a letter home,
His father waited for his younger son.

Continued

The months passed by, the money soon was done,
The cars were sold, and all his friends had gone,
Reduced to shame, his roof the sky above,
"I'll go back home, back to my father's love
Yes, I'll go home, my family is there,
I'll take a servant's job, a servant's share."

"Forgive me father, please," he tried to say,
But love and joy forbade the words that day.
New clothes, new shoes, a ring, a feast prepared,
His father welcomed home this son who'd erred,
Forgiveness free was given, quite unearned,
In love he'd waited for his son's return.

Our Father God is waiting for His sons
Who've wandered far away fast bound in sin.
His arms outstretched in love upon the cross,
He suffered, died, and rose again for us.
Oh hungry, thirsty, weary, lost in sin,
Your heavenly Father's waiting your return.

The Dream

Scenes from the Life of Jesus Christ, to be found in the New Testament. Luke 4:16-22, John :1-14, Luke 19:29-40, Luke 22:39-48, Luke 22:54-62, Matthew 27:11-24, John 19:17, Luke 22:33-34

I went to church as usual that day,
I sang the hymns and also knelt to pray,
I listened to the reading from God's Word,
I heard it speak of Jesus Christ the Lord,
I saw the preacher climb the pulpit steps
The church was warm, I settled back and slept!

I stood inside a church in Nazareth,
I heard him read the lesson from Esias,
I saw Him close the book and then sit down,
I watched the people sitting round Him frown,
I listened to their words when He had done,
They said, "We know this man, He's Jesus, Joseph's Son."

I sat among five thousand on a hill.
I shared the loaves and fishes, ate my fill,
I watched Him heal the sick and blind and lame,
I heard Him gently speak to all who came,
I asked of one who'd had his sight restored,
"Who is this Man?" The answer was, "The Lord."

I saw Him ride the colt from Bethany,
I walked beside the people there that day,
I helped to spread palm branches on the ground,
I heard hosannas ring from all around,
I asked, "Who is this Man whose praise you sing?"
They answered, "Jesus Christ our future King."

I found myself in dark Gethsemane,
I heard Him pray in deepest agony,
I saw His blood drip on the ground as sweat,
I sat beside His followers as they slept,
He said, as Judas hailed Him with a kiss,
"Would you betray the Son of Man like this?"   *Continued*

101

I stood with Peter in the High Priest's hall,
I heard him say, "I don't know Him at all."
I winced as soldiers split his back with whips,
I watched as Pilate washed his hands of guilt,
I heard him ask his prisoner, "Who are You,
Are You as they accuse, King of the Jews?"

I saw Him drag the cross up Calvary,
I was among the crowd that thronged the way,
I heard their shouts and jeers as He fell down,
I saw the blood drip from His head thorn crowned,
I asked those standing near, "What has He done?"
The answer was, "He claimed to be God's Son."

I stood beside that cross on Calvary,
I watched the soldiers nail Him to the tree,
I heard Him whisper, "Father, forgive their sin,"
I saw the darkness fall and cover Him,
I woke and found myself there in my pew,
The preacher asking, "What is this Man to You?"

"What is this Man to You?" the preacher asked,
"Is He just Joseph's son from Nazareth,
Is He the One Who multiplied the bread
So that five thousand people were all fed,
Or is He Jesus, Saviour, King of Kings,
Whose death bought us forgiveness for our sins?"

Who Are You?

Luke 18: 8-14

Two men went into the temple that day,
Both of them Jews, both going to pray.
One was a Pharisee, clever and pious,
The other a Publican, a collector of taxes.
Each in his own way was seeking for God.
One was sincere, and one was a fraud.

"Look at me, Lord," the Pharisee prayed,
"I'm a good man, Lord, all my tithes have been paid,
I fast twice in the week, I'm not evil, like some,
Lying, cheating and stealing, I've never done.
Thank You O God, that I'm a good man,
Just look over there Lord, at that Publican."

The Publican stood afar off, on his own,
Head bent, in despair, eyes fixed on the ground.
"Forgive me, O God, forgive me my sin,
Be merciful Lord, and cleanse me within;
Take over my life, and change every part,
I'm lost without You Lord, come into my heart."

Our Lord told this story to men of His day
Who thought they were righteous, had no need to pray.
Had no need of God, were proud of their deeds,
Thought they'd get them to heaven, ignored others' needs.
He made it quite plain, man must acknowledge his sin,
Confess before God, ask the Saviour within.

So many today live self-satisfied lives,
Go to church every Sunday and even pay tithes.
Pat themselves on the back, point the finger at others
Who've fallen in sin, forget men are brothers,
Forget God has said, in His word unto men,
"Return unto Me and be born again."

Continued

My friends, have you given your heart to the Lord,
Do you know His forgiveness and trust in His word?
Have you peace in your soul, does He fill all your needs,
Or are you relying on salvation by deeds?
You can't save your soul by the things that you do,
Jesus died on the cross, gave His life to save you.

The Hungry Ones

Did you see them that night, on News at Ten
Caught by the camera in all their despair,
Babies and toddlers, old women, old men,
Framed on the screen, brought to us there
In our warm living rooms, as we sat at ease
Sipping our coffee, or drinking our tea?

Great eyes looking straight into our lives
From little skull heads, pot bellies, stick legs.
Hunger, starvation, before our eyes
In Karamoja, Ugnanda, they plead and they beg
"Give us something to eat before we all die.
Have mercy, send help," they mournfully cry.

Great black flies on a little child's face.
Three small boys pick dried meal off a bin.
The camera takes us from place to place
Showing more swollen black bellies, arms and legs thin
With hunger so raw we can't take it in.
Our little fellow attempts a weak grin!

Did you see that programme on News at Ten?
What did you do, switch off, forget them?
Or did you miss a meal, count the cost and then
Send the money to feed even one of those kids
You saw starving and dying of hunger, in pain,
Or - did you do nothing, again?

She Loved Him

She Loved Him or Poured Out

Luke 7:47

The story of Mary is told in each of the four gospels.
Thomas A. Kempis wrote:-
"Whatsoever is done of love, be it ever so little and con-
temptible in the sight of the world, becomes wholly fruitful.
For God weighs more the love out of which a man works
than the work which he does. He does much who loves
much. He who has true and perfect love seeks himself in
nothing, but only desires in all things the glory of God".
M.R. De Haan wrote:-
"Do you as a Christian attract others by your gracious words
and deeds, and the sanctifying aroma of the indwelling
Christ? The ointment Mary spent on her Saviour filled the
whole house!"

Simon had come to me, late the previous night,
With news of Jesus, He was coming back
To Bethany, our dearest Friend, our Lord,
Was coming back to us, He'd sent us word.
And so we planned a feast for all our guests,
Simon and Mary helped and Lazarus,
Whom Jesus raised from death to life again.
Jesus was coming here with all His friends.

We baked, set tables, worked all morning long
Preparing food; I did it with a song,
Because the Lord had taught me that my job,
Done cheerfully, brought glory to our God.
Mary, my dearest sister, did the flowers,
Patiently working through the hottest hours.
She'd turned quite pale when Simon spread the news
Of Jesus' visit to the waiting Jews.

Mary was sensitive towards the Lord,
She seemed to understand His every word.
Once I was angry when she spent her hours
Listening to Jesus; then, He showed His power
By raising brother Lazarus from the grave.
He wept with us; I saw His power to save.
"He that believes on Me shall never die",
He told me then; and so I love Him now.

Mary was quiet through the busy day.
She still looked pale, had nothing much to say.
The work all done, she slipped into her room,
I saw her lift her box of sweet perfume,
Her precious box, which gave her so much pleasure,
Her alabaster box, her dearest treasure.
Her tears fell fast, as over it she bent,
I moved away, not know what they meant.

Soon all was done, we hadn't long to wait.
The cheers, outside, told Christ was at the gate.
He entered Simon's house and took a seat,
Weary from walking in the noon-day heat.
We served the meal, and all enjoyed the feast,
I was too occupied to notice much
Of what was going on, or what was said,
Until a silence fell; I raised my head.

I saw my sister Mary just a pace
Behind the Lord, tears streaming down her face.
Between her hands her box of perfume sweet,
And, as I watched, she poured it o'er His feet.
I couldn't move was rooted to my feet.
Then Jesus spoke a quiet word to her
Before loud voices broke upon the air.

Continued

Judas Iscariot, not noted for his tact,
With angry words denounced the lovely act.
"This perfume, wasted here, should have been sold,
The money given to the poor and old."
Jesus looked hard at Judas, then He said,
"The poor you'll have with you when I am dead.
From this day, Mary's deed will be made known,
The world, much richer, by the love she's shown."

Mary poured out her all to Christ that day,
She showed her love in this, so special, way.
Her precious ointment, broken o'er His feet,
Filled the whole room and made her deed complete.
Have you poured out your all before the Lord,
Your precious treasures, all you are, in love
To Him, whose blood poured out on Calvary,
That we, to Him, a sweet perfume may be?

Bartimaeus

Mark 10:46-52

Day after day, he had sat there
In the dust of a Jericho street,
Blind eyes useless, but pleading,
Ears strained for the passing of feet.
Rags covered his poor, filthy body,
Dirty arms reach upwards for alms,
"Please, help me", whined blind Bartimaeus,
But few coins dropped into his hands.

Year after wearisome year passed,
His pleadings were largely ignored,
People were used to his presence,
And he learned a lot from their words.
He heard of the deaths and the weddings,
Of whose daughter had married whose son,
He knew who was sick, or disabled,
But he sat there, blind and alone.

Then one day, he picked up some gossip,
A tid-bit, beyond all belief,
For it had to do with Zacchaeus,
A publican, rich, but a thief.
Many a time he had passed him
On his way to the tax gatherer's seat,
But never a coin came from Zacchaeus,
Though he'd pleaded for something to eat.

Now, he heard that Zacchaeus was different,
Had changed, become a new man.
He'd returned, more than double the money
To people he'd cheated and harmed.
What had happened to Zacchaeus?
A miracle must have been done.
Someone spoke of a man called Jesus,
He was there in Zacchaeus' home.

Continued

Who was this man they called Jesus?
The blind man sat in deep thought
In some way He'd changed old Zacchaeus,
A miracle, yes, then He thought
To be able to help him, Bartimaeus,
Who was weary of life in the streets.
Who was this man they called Jesus,
Was it possible that they could meet?

Next morning he heard many voices,
Crowds shouting, feet running, much talk,
Again, of the Man they called Jesus.
It seemed, that today, He would walk
Right past poor, blind Bartimaeus,
Right past him, and out of his life.
This Jesus had changed old Zacchaeus,
He could surely give him back his sight.

The people were pushing and shoving,
How could he make his voice heard?
"Please, help me, Jesus", he shouted.
But the crowds only laughed at his words.
"Be quiet, blind man, you're a nuisance,
The Master has no time for you."
But he shouted the more, "Son of David,
Have mercy on me, please do."

Amid all the noise Jesus heard him,
The shrill voice calling His name,
And he sent for blind Bartimaeus,
Who arose, left his rags, and came
And knelt in the dust, there before Him,
His poor eyes, black as the night,
"What will I do for you, blind man?" asked Jesus.
"Lord, please give me back my sight."

Continued

Jesus looked with compassion upon him,
This poor man, pleading but bold.
He spoke, in love, to him, gently,
"Bartimaeus, your faith makes you whole."
He lifted his eyes to the Saviour,
Darkness had fled, all was light,
And he followed the Man they call Jesus,
Who had given him back his sight.

Are you walking alone in the darkness?
Is each day a burden to you?
Cast your care on the Man they call Jesus,
He'll make your life over anew.
The Saviour will lighten your darkness,
He'll give you a vision that's clear.
The Light of the World has the answer.
Turn to Him now, He will hear.

Zacchaeuss

Luke 19:1-10

Before the day, that day that changed my life,
I lived alone, no family, no wife,
No one to care whether I lived or died.
The government employed me. On the side
I found that I could grow quite rich
By overcharging people on their tax.
The Romans got their dues, they didn't care,
But I was shunned by all Jews everywhere.

At first, I didn't let it bother me.
I lived well, pretended not to see
Men draw aside whenever I appeared.
The children followed me and laughed and jeered
And called me names, because I was so small.
My riches didn't comfort me at all.
My life was bleak, my conscience troubled me,
Then, Jesus came and I climbed up the tree.

Yes, Jesus came to Jericho that day.
The crowds pushed past me down the narrow way.
All of them curious to see this Man
Whose fame had spread before Him through the land.
I'd heard the gossip in the dusty streets
About this Jesus, and I longed to meet Him.
They said He'd made a beggarman to see.
I wondered, could He change my life for me?

Being a small man meant I could not see
Above the crowds and so I climbed the tree
To get a better view as He passed by.
He wouldn't bother much with such as I,
A publican, rejected by the Jews
Because I'd taken more than was my due,
And so, I did not understand at all
When Jesus stopped and I heard my name called.

Continued

He stopped and looked up into the tree,
"Come down, Zacchaeus, please", He said to me,
"Today I plan to stay a while with you".
Amazement showed among the gathered Jews.
"He's going to eat with him, a sinner,
That publican, that thief, that tax-gatherer."
On every face their thoughts were plain to read,
But Jesus looked at me and saw my need.

The Son of God came to my house that day.
He spoke to me gently and so lovingly,
The darkness left my soul, I was set free,
But still my guilty conscience troubled me.
"Lord, I have taken much from many men,
I will give back fourfold to all of them,
For Lord, I want to love and follow you
The Saviour, Who has made my life anew."

That day, the Son of God became my guest.
I welcomed Him, with joy, unto the feast.
He said He'd come to seek and save the lost.
I didn't know what it was going to cost
Him, until later, when He died on Calvary.
Jesus, the Son of God, sought and saved me,
Forgave my guilty past and set me free,
And all because, that day, I climbed a tree.

Zacchaeus climbed a tree in Jericho.
Because of this he got to know
The Son of God, his life was made anew,
This little man, this publican, this Jew.
Our Saviour climbed the hill of Calvary
And died upon a tree for you and me.
And still He seeks the sinner, high and low,
As He did long ago, in Jericho.

The Storm

Mark 4:35-41

Lake Galilee lay calm in evening light.
The last sunrays made paths, shining and bright
To where, with busy hands, the old men sat
Mending their nets, tongues occupied with chat.
Only the seabirds' cries broke the deep peace,
And gentle waves lapping the sandy beach.

Father along the shore a group of men
Stood round their boats, they numbered nine or ten.
All afternoon they'd been besieged by crowds
Seeking the Lord, Peter and Andrew proud
That He had used their boat from which to preach.
Now, weary and tired, they pushed off from the beach.

The boat put out from shore into the deep.
Jesus, tired out, lay down and fell asleep.
Peter and Andrew, seasoned fishermen,
Anxiously scanned the sky for weather signs.
Strong winds began to blow, the sea to rise,
The sky drew dark, the waves increased in size.

Peter had never seen a storm so wild
Upon the lake he'd known well from a child.
Thunder began to crack and lightning flashed,
The boat shipped water, its useless rudder crashed.
There, in the stern, the Lord slept. On and on
The storm raged, the mast went overboard, the sails had
gone!

Upon the mountainous waves the boat was tossed.
The brothers clung in fear, sure all was lost.
Then Peter found his voice and yelled his fear,
"The storm is raging, Master, do you hear?
Jesus, wake up and save us or we'll drown,
Oh, save us Lord, the ship is going down!"

Continued

Jesus stood up and slowly looked around.
His eyes took in the sight, His ears the sound
Of raging waves, of roaring, mighty wind,
Of His disciples fear; His look was kind,
His voice was gentle; "Quiet waves, be still."
The storm died down, obedient to His will.

Peter and Andrew, their faces, pale with fear,
Stared at the Lord as, calmly, He stood there.
"Where is your faith my friends and why this fear?"
The Master asked, "Why fear when I am near?"
"Who is this man?" Peter was heard to say,
"Who is this Man the elements obey?"

Are you afraid when storms begin to blow?
Does your faith fail and drag your spirits low?
Do you forget that Jesus said, He cares?
He's in life's boat with you and waits to share
Your roughest voyage. He's there through good and ill.
In gentle tones He's saying, "Peace, be still."

The Thankful One

Luke 17: 11-19

My friends and I suffered from leprosy,
Outcasts, we lived upon the countryside.
Though they were Jews and I, Samaritan,
Our common suffering triumphed over pride.
Nobody knew or cared that we were homeless,
We lived in caves, avoided being seen,
Our dread disease was feared and loathed by all men.
If one approached we had to cry, "Unclean."

Life seemed to all of us a living prison,
No hope of healing brightened dreary days,
Outcast from home and family made us bitter,
God seemed to shut His ears to all our prayers.
But then, one day, I heard a bit of gossip,
A man, a Jew, living in Galilee,
Was healing men of all kinds of diseases,
We wondered, could He heal our leprosy?

Many and varied stories of His doings,
His miracles, His words, His loving deeds,
Reached us and raised our hopes that He could heal us,
Restore us to our homes and meet our need.
Rumour said, He was coming to the borders
Of Galilee and of Samaria,
He must pass close to us, in isolation.
Would He come near us, outcasts, would He care?

He came that day, we met Him on the highway.
We called to Him from where we stood, afar,
"Have mercy, Master, please, have mercy on us,"
Thinking that now He would display His power.
He did not raise His hands, do any action
That would have shown us that He cared, at least
We did not see Him, but we heard His order,
"Go to the town, show yourselves to the priest".

Continued

Surprised, we turned to carry out His order,
All, like us, who were cured, had this to do,
And, as we went, amazement grew between us,
For each of us was healed and made anew.
We saw the priest, who certified us healthy.
The others, full of joy, went on their way.
I turned to follow them but then, remembered
The One Whose word had healed us all that day.

I found Him, as He travelled to Jerusalem,
And knelt before Him, glorifying God
And giving thanks to Jesus Who had healed me
Because, by faith, I had obeyed His word.
"Where are the other nine?" He asked me, gently,
"Have they no thanks to give to God above?
Only this stranger, this Samaritan
Returns to show his gratitude and love."

Jesus reached out His hand and gently raised me
To stand before Him, whole and made anew.
"Return now to your home and be my witness,"
He said, "Tell others what the Lord has done for you."
And so, I tell you now about the Saviour,
His loving kindness reaches to all men.
Obey Him, praise Him, thank Him for His goodness,
As did this outcast, this Samaritan.

The First Miracle

John 2:1-11

Why did they have to kill my dearest Lord?
I stood in Pilate's court and heard them roar
"Crucify, this Man is not our King."
And, as I waited there, I saw them bring
My Saviour out, upon His back, a cross.
I felt I could not cope with such a loss,
But as my Jesus passed He looked at me
And I remembered Cana, Galilee.

My cousin Jonas lived in Galilee.
His family was very good to me.
I was the 'poor relation,' but they shared
Their home with me. To show how much I cared
I worked all day and far into the night,
Sometimes awake to see dawn's early light.
But oh, my heart held only bitterness
And my sharp tongue brought loved ones much distress.

Because of this, they left me on my own
And I began to spend my time alone.
I understood their feelings but I found
The more I tried, more hurt spread around.
I was frustrated, what was I to do?
As hour by hour anger and sadness grew.
Then, one glad day, Jesus of Nazareth came,
My life was made anew, my heart was changed.

A marriage was arranged for Jonas' son.
The plans prepared and ticked off one by one.
The food was ordered, jars of wine brought in,
If this ran short, disgrace was brought on him.
The morning dawned, the guests had all arrived,
Then, we received some unexpected news,
Jesus had come with a small band of Jews.

Continued

What would we do? The wine was almost gone!
I went to Mary, she went to her Son.
What could He do, this Man from Nazareth?
My thoughts were scornful, I was lacking faith.
Mary brought Jesus to the kitchen door,
He looked quite ordinary, robes clean but poor.
But when I looked into those loving eyes
My heart was cleansed of all pretence and lies.

It was as though my soul was laid quite bare,
And He could see all that was buried there.
I felt as though a load had rolled away,
There was no need for tears, nor words to say.
Mary spoke softly, as the silence grew,
"Whatever my Son says unto you, do."
His order tried my new found faith in Him,
"Fill every water pot up to the brim."

We did as we were told, but doubtfully.
What would old Jonas say to us this day
When he poured water out, instead of wine?
But Jesus' look assured me all was fine.
We watched the guests as the fresh drink was poured,
My heart rejoiced as their comments were heard.
Surprise and pleasure showed in the looks they cast,
"Jonas, you've kept the best wine to the last."

'That miracle was Jesus' first,' they say.
But I'm a walking miracle today.
His look of love cleansed me from all my sin
And He has died that all may come to Him.
He'll give you power to live and overcome
All of your problems, you are not alone.
When Jesus bids you put your trust in Him
He'll fill your life with new wine, to the brim.

Deaf and Dumb

Matthew 7:31-37

It was Matthew who told us of Jesus.
His story was hard to believe,
But the proof was there, living before us,
He certainly could not deceive.
For, his life was a constant reminder
That something had happened to him.
He claimed that One, Jesus of Nazareth,
Had freed him from demons and sin.

We just had to believe him, for Matthew,
Who had lived a violent life,
Was a walking example of healing,
No devil possession, no strife.
This Jesus had cast out his demons,
He'd sent Matthew home to proclaim
The good news of a wonderful Saviour,
Who could save men from sin and from shame.

Because Matthew had told us of Jesus
And what He had done for his soul,
We decided that Simon should see Him,
This Jesus could make our friend whole.
Since birth he'd been deaf as a doorpost,
All alone in a silent world.
His speech was confused and he stammered,
Unable to make himself heard.

Jesus came to the district, one morning.
Crowds gathered, curious to see
What He'd do for the sick and disabled,
For the sinbound, needing set free.
With Simon, we stood there and watched Him
As, gently, He touched everyone.
The blind received his sight, the paralysed walked,
And then, we found, our turn had come.

Continued

Jesus looked with compassion on Simon,
Then, taking him by the hand,
He led him away from the people
To the edge of a piece of waste land.
We saw Him make signs to Simon,
Put His fingers into his ears,
Then He touched his tongue with saliva,
Sighed, looked up to heaven and prayed.

We could see Simon watch Jesus closely,
He understood all that He did.
With sign language Jesus had shown him.
Then, "Ephphatha, Be opened", He said.
Immediately Simon looked startled,
In wonder he lifted his head,
He seemed to be listening carefully,
Then, "I can hear, I can speak," he cried.

We rejoiced with our dear friend Simon,
Who praised God with his new speech.
He told everyone who would listen,
And took them to hear Jesus teach.
He listened to each word of Jesus,
Rejoicing in every sound.
We joined him in praising the Saviour
In Whom his healing was found.

Are you deaf to the voice of the Saviour?
Can you hear Him above the world's din?
What kind of a witness are you, friend?
Does your speech bring honour to Him?
The Saviour can open your ears, friend,
That you may give heed to His word.
He'll loosen your tongue to tell others
Of our wonderful, glorious Lord.

He Meets Our Need

Matthew 12:1-13

The synagogue was filled, right to the door,
With Pharisees and priests, with rich and poor,
All waiting in expectancy to see
Jesus of Nazareth: rumour said that He
Was coming to the service there that day
And that He'd passed through corn fields on the way.
The Pharisees were angry, said that He'd
Allowed His followers to gather seed
And eat it, breaking thus the Sabbath law.
So now, they watched Him, critical of all they saw.

There, seated in the midst, was a poor man
Who, all his life, had had a withered hand.
He could not move it, lacking any power
To lift it, he had suffered greatly, more
From taunts and jeers than any inconvenience.
He'd heard how Jesus healed the blind and lame, hence
His presence in the synagogue to see
If Christ would notice him and maybe He
Would heal him, though it was the Sabbath day.
Now rumour said that He was on His way.

He came into the church and there sat down,
Aware of all the Pharisees around
Waiting to see what He would say or do,
Trying to catch Him out on points of law.
But Jesus saw the man in all his need,
His lack of power, his weakness, and no creed
Or law could keep the Christ from making whole
A lifeless hand; He called this needy soul,
And stood him in the midst of all those men,
And, with a word, He healed him there and then.

Continued

Our Lord can see our need, yes, yours and mine,
It matters not the month, or day, or time,
Or man's objections on a point of creed.
He waits for us to recognise our need,
Our helplessness, our weakness and our sin
Which is forgiven when we turn to Him,
Who, by His death on Calvary's cruel tree,
Purchased our pardon, made us whole and free.
He meets our every need, He is our Lord,
Lord of our heart, Lord of our thoughts, and Lord of every
word.

The Saviour and the Judge

Romans 14:10

Traffic was lighter than usual
Down the length of the motorway,
As the judge drove quickly homeward
After a busy day.
His thoughts were still in the courtroom,
Faces still crowing his mind,
When a car shot quickly past him,
"Young fool, he ought to be fined".

Farther ahead, on the highway,
He saw the same car again,
Swerving and skidding quite badly
And weaving from lane to lane.
"What on earth does he think he's doing?
He's driving like someone insane."
Then, the judge saw the car overturning
And suddenly burst into flames.

He stopped his own car quickly
And ran to the young man's aid,
He managed to pull the door open
Expecting to find him dead.
The man was alive and conscious,
The judge pulled him out of the car,
The young man was very grateful,
"You saved my life, thank you, Sir."

Many years passed in the courthouse,
Then, one day, a prisoner appeared
Charged with the crime of murder,
The judge was one to be feared.
The evidence proved the man guilty,
The judge placed the black cap on his head.
The sentence pronounced was final,
"You'll be handed, by the neck, 'till you're dead."

Continued

The prisoner spoke, in a whisper,
"Do you not remember?" he said,
"How you saved me from death on the highway
One day, when my car was in flames.
How can you pronounce the death sentence
On one whose life you once saved?
Have mercy on me," begged the prisoner.
The judge answered with words that were grave.

"That day on the highway, I saved you
And gave you your life again,
But it seems that you didn't used it,
You've brought much sorrow and pain."
The prisoner pleaded for mercy
But the magistrate did not budge.
He said, "On that day I was your saviour,
Today I am your judge."

The moments are passing swiftly
And the Saviour is waiting still
For sinners to find forgiveness
At the cross on Calvary's hill.
But soon, this life will be ended,
Our Lord will be coming again,
If today He is not your Saviour,
He'll be sitting as your Judge then.

The Jailer

Acts 16:16-34

For many years I'd lived at Philippi,
My dearest wife, my family and I.
I was the keeper of the local jail
Which kept me busy, yet it failed
To bring me peace of mind or any joy.
The Roman government, in whose employ
I spent my life, was cruel, stern and cold.
I served it well and did as I was told.

Many a time I wished that life would change,
Day followed day and things remained the same.
Prisoners of all kinds seemed to come and go,
Many were beaten, others killed, I know,
I was ashamed; some of the things I saw
Done to those men; but that was Roman law!
I could not disobey by word or deed,
I had a wife and family to feed.

One day, two men, Silas and Paul, by name
Were brought to me in jail, they were the same
Men I had seen earlier that day
Accosted by a girl along the way,
Crying, "These men are servants of the Most High God
Bringing to us salvation from the Lord."
(This girl was said to be possessed, insane,
She brought her masters much by way of gain).

One of the men appeared greatly concerned.
The girl kept crying after them, he turned
And raised his arms above the girl and said,
"In Jesus' name I now command you, go."
The evil spirit fled.
The girl, released, was quiet and at peace.
Her masters, seeing their profit gone were quite irate
And dragged the men before the magistrates.

Continued

Silas and Paul were flogged and thrown in jail,
And I was warned, that if I failed
To keep them safely I would lose my life.
I thought of home, my family, my wife,
And thrust the men into the inner cell,
And chained their feet fast in the stocks as well.
Their backs were bruised and bleeding, very sore,
They smiled at me before I locked the door.

Later that night, I scarce believed my ears,
Those men were singing songs, the prisoners all could hear them,
Songs of praise unto their God,
And praying too and calling on their Lord;
Those men, who had been flogged that very day,
Were praising God, and yes, I heard them pray
For me and all the men imprisoned there,
Unto their God, as though He knew and cared.

Who was this God Who could inspired such praise?
I envied them the faith which thus could raise
Songs and prayer, there in the midst of pain.
Who was the God they praised and praised again?
I heard them call Him Saviour, Jesus, Lord
And all the other prisoners heard their words.
They said that He had died upon a tree
To save all men from sin. Could this mean me?

Weary and sad, I went to bed and slept,
Certain that all were locked and safely kept
There in the cells; but then, about midnight
An earthquake started. Shaking with fright
I stumbled from my bed, stones fell around,
The noise was deafening, the walls fell down,
The prison doors burst open, chains were snapped,
I was confused; the prisoners had escaped!

Continued

Scared out of my wits I drew my sword to kill myself.
But then, within the cell I heard these words,
"Do yourself no harm, we are all here."
Was it a dream? Trembling with fear
I called for lights and ran into the cell,
Fell on my knees before the men, "Please tell
Me how I can be saved," I begged.
"Believe on Jesus Christ," they said.

I took them to my home and washed their stripes.
They spoke to us of God. That very night
We all believed on Christ the Crucified,
Rejoiced and praised the Lord and were baptised.
Do you praise Him when everything goes wrong?
Do you despair, or lift your voice in song?
Do you know God, Whom Paul and Silas praised
Amid the pain and suffering of that jail?

My Cross

John 19:17

I read the story, from which I got the idea for this poem, in
Mr.s Cowman's Streams in the Desert!

"Take up thy cross and follow Me," Christ said.
I sought, each day, to follow where He led.
The years flew past and with their ebb and flow
My spirit dragged, my burdens seemed to grow
Daily more heavy, there was none to care.
"Oh Lord," I cried, "this cross I cannot bear.
Why should I have to work so very hard
While others, rich already, reap rewards,
And spend their lives in happy, carefree ways?
No heavy crosses burden them each day."

Tired out, one night, I went to bed and slept,
My mind exhausted with the tears I'd wept.
My sleep was broken, 'till at last, it seemed,
A vision formed before me in a dream.
I found myself where many crosses lay,
Some large, some small; I saw that each one varied
From its neighbour; some beautiful; some grey
And plain; some bound with lovely flowers, I prayed,
"Lord, let me choose my cross from one of these."
He answered, "Choose, My child, take any one you please."

I looked at all those crosses lying there,
And then, I saw one, beautiful and fair,
Studded with diamonds, rubies, set in gold.
"This I can wear in comfort, I can mould
It to my needs," I pondered in my dream.
I stopped to lift that cross, but then, it seemed,
My body bent beneath its heavy load,
I couldn't take one step upon the road.
"Oh Lord," I cried, "It's much too hard to bear,
This jewelled cross will weigh me down, I fear."

Continued

I looked around again and then I saw
Another, lighter cross, without a flaw.
Rich carvings cut it deep and flowers entwined
About its slender form; I could not find
One fault with it. And then, I lifted it.
That flowery cross, so lovely to the eye,
When taken up, drew from me a loud cry.
The flowers entwined around it hid sharp thorns,
My poor hands grasping it were scratched and torn.
"Oh Lord," I cried, "this cross cannot be borne."

Then, in my dream, I saw one, plain and grey,
Lying alone upon the dusty way.
No jewels shone from it, no flowers entwined.
Only some words were written there in lines.
I stooped to read its message from above,
A message written there in words of love.
"Take up this cross, My child, for it is yours,
Though it looks dull and grey and very poor,
I know which cross is best for you to bear,
I fashioned it with loving thought and care.
I bore my cross for you to Calvary,
Take up your cross and bear it now, for Me."

I took my cross again from His dear hand,
It still looked dull, not beautiful and grand.
But, as I lifted it, a radiance shone
Upon it from above, its pain had gone.
It fitted my weak form, God made it so,
And in His strength I now, rejoicing, go.
We do not know what crosses others bear,
We envy them, their lives seem rich and fair.
But heavy crosses are by others borne,
If we could choose, we'd gladly choose our own.

The Cross Leads Home

There is a popular gospel hymn which has, as its chorus,
these words:
The way of the cross leads home,
The way of the cross leads home,
It is sweet to know, as I onward go,
The way of the cross leads home.

Johnnie held tightly to his mother's hand,
Crowds thronged the busy streets, the shop was jammed
With jostling people, adults towered above him,
Pushed against him; he was sore in every limb.
"Wish mother would go home", poor Johnnie thought,
"Then I could play with that toy car she bought."

Johnnie looked up, and then he looked around.
Where was his mum? She wasn't to be found;
What would he do? She might be at the door;
Johnnie searched every counter, every floor
With no success, his mum had disappeared
And he was lost and feeling very scared.

The street was noisy, busses everywhere,
But he was lost and no-one seemed to care.
He did not know which bus would take him home.
Johnnie was frightened, very much alone.
He sat down on the kerb to rest his feet,
Along came a policeman on his beat.

Johnnie gazed up into his gentle eyes.
He seemed so kind that he began to cry,
"Oh sir, I'm lost and no-one seems to know
Where my dear mummy is and I've searched high and low.
I just can't find her. I let go her hand.
I looked all through the shop, then went to stand
Beside the door; it was no use,
I think she must have gone home to our house."

Continued

The big policeman took him in his arms,
Glad that he hadn't come to any harm.
"Do you know where you live? I'll take you home,
You'll soon be safely back there with your mum."
"Oh sir, my mother said if I was lost
That's I'd get home by starting at The Cross".

Have you, like Johnnie, lost your way today?
Have you let go Christ's hand and gone astray?
You're wandering in confusion, darkness, sin,
The path back home is known only to Him.
In gentle tones He says, "My lost child, come,
Start at the cross and it will lead you home."

In The Midst

There are many words of comfort in the Bible,
Which mean many different things to those who read,
For the Holy Spirit opens up the scriptures
And lights up a word for every person's need.
When you come across a 'now familiar' passage
You look forward to the message that it brings,
For the word of God gives hope and peace and guidance,
Lighting up the way and making your heart sing.

There's a group of words, repeated in the gospels,
Which tells us that the Lord of all is near.
We are told that, where His people meet together,
He's 'in the midst' to guide and help and cheer.
'In the midst,' yes, Christ is always present
Where His people meet to worship and to pray.
Are you aware He's with you, there beside you,
Every moment, every hour, of every day?

That day, upon the lovely Lake of Galilee,
The awful storm caused fear in every breast,
And yet, there in the stern lay Christ the Saviour
'In the midst', a peaceful figure, taking rest.
The winds of life may blow about your vessel
And waves may threaten to o'er flow your boat,
If Christ is 'in the midst' you need not fear them,
His 'peace be still,' will bring you safe to port.

Three crosses were prepared on Calvary's mountain
For criminals, deserving of this death.
Two thieves hung there, on either side the centre,
And 'in the midst' the Son of God was placed.
For our iniquities, the Saviour suffered,
He shed His blood upon that cruel tree,
There 'in the midst' of enemies and sinners
He gave His life, in love, to set us free.

Continued

136

He came unto His own and they refused Him,
As, 'in the midst,' He stood one Sabbath day,
But passing 'through their midst' He left them, standing,
They spurned the Lord and He went on His way.
Our Saviour's 'in the midst' this very moment,
He's standing at the door of every heart.
If you refuse to open to His knocking
He may pass 'through the midst' and then depart.

The Light in the Window

This poem was inspired by a true story. In America, during
the First World War, candles were placed in the windows of
homes where a son or husband had been killed.

The small boy curled up in the window-seat,
Watching the lights coming on in the street.
In some of the houses candles were lit,
Looking like stars in the dark of the night.
The small boy looked out at the candleglow,
"Mummy," he called, "I would like to know
Why there are candles in some of those homes,
Yet in others, like ours, there are none?"

His mother lifted the boy on her knee,
Put her arm round him, "Now, listen to me,
I'll tell you the story why candles are lit
In some of the houses you see in the street.
In each of those homes, where you see a light,
A son was a soldier who died, in the fight
To keep our world free from evil and sin,
The candlelight shows we remember him."

The small boy curled up in the window again,
Counting the candles, his thoughts on the men
Whose lives had been given that he might be free.
"They did it for mummy and daddy and me."
He lifted his eyes and saw, in the sky,
A star shining brightly, and gave a glad cry,
"Mummy," he called, "come here, come and see,
God's Son must have died so that we could be free."

The little boy's mother sat down by his side.
"Yes, my son, it is good news, God's Son has died
For you and for me and for men everywhere.
Our sins are forgiven. By His death we share
In the promise of heaven. God's Son is alive,
He has fought the good fight, the battle is won
When we love Him and trust Him with our lives, my son."

So Are Ye In My Hand

Jeremiah 18:1-6

I find this passage very comforting. When we fail it is good to know that our Lord does not cast us aside as useless. He will perfect that which concerneth us. (Psalm 138:8).

The people crowded round the potter's wheel
As he created there, with grace and skill,
A vessel, beautiful in shape and form,
Before their eyes; a lovely vase was born
Between the potter's hands. His touch was sure,
Making from clay a vessel to endure.

The vase took shape as o'er the wheel he bent,
Steadily moulding, shaping, eyes intent
Upon his work; but then I heard a gasp
Come from the crowd and, looking past
Them, saw the new formed vase was marred
There in the potter's hand; we stood and stared.

What would he do? The perfect shape was spoiled.
The potter's perfect plan for it was foiled.
The vase, broken in many pieces, lay
Between his hands, just useless clay.
We waited, sure he'd cast it all aside
And start with new, that clay had failed when tried.

We watched; again the potter took the clay
Firmly into his hands and laid
It, gently, on the wheel, before our eyes.
Accompanied then by our admiring cries
That poor, marred clay was formed, by his sure hand,
Into a vessel, beautiful and grand.

Continued

The prophet Jeremiah, took a walk,
He tells us, down to the potter's shop
And there, the Lord showed him what we had seen;
A vessel, made of clay, which too had been
Marred in the potter's hand and made again
"So are ye in My hand," the Lord told him.

"So are ye in My hand," said God the Lord.
But we, the clay, may thwart His precious word.
The hands which mould us bear the marks of nails,
And He will hold us, He will never fail.
He seeks to perfect us by His great love
Which worketh our salvation from above.

No Miracles

John 10:41

The idea for this poem came from F. B. Meyer's "Our Daily
Walk." Reading for September 27th.

"The age of miracles is past," men say,
"The world does not believe such things today.
They may have happened once, not any more,
Men have outgrown these stories, this folklore.
Mankind is now mature and childish things
Are put away – no miracles today."

But – last Spring, from bulbs which looked quite dead,
Came snowdrops, white, with dancing heads,
And daffodils and crocus flowers
Of every hue, which show His power
To make anew from tiny seeds
Such wond'rous beauty – no miracles today!

But – last Autumn, farmers gathered grain
To feed the world, the sun and raid
Were sent by God to make it grow.
The farmer reaped it, row by row.
God can turn water into wine
And change the sky from blue to grey – no miracles today?

What do you say? Do you see miracles today?
A word from you, when used by God,
Can change a life, only one word
Or one deed done, can lead a soul to God's own Son.
Allow the Lord your life to fill
And men will see a miracle.

Broken Pieces

John 6:12 RV

This poem was jotted down on the back of an envelope one
evening in February 1982. It came straight from the Lord at
a time when many problems were piling up.
The idea of the 'broken pieces' was in my mind from the
reading for January 25th, in Amy Carmichael's "Edges of
His Ways."

What are your thoughts, when you lie down to sleep,
At the end of a busy day?
How do you feel when you think of the things
You wish you'd not done and not said?
You started the day with a prayer on your lips
And committed each moment to Him,
But now, looking back, you have nothing to bring,
Only failure and sadness and sin.

"O Lord, I have failed You, again and again,
I started the day with such joy,
But somehow, somewhere in the rush and work
I found only things to annoy.
I forgot about love when I spoke that harsh word,
I forgot to be gentle and kind,
I forgot to be patient with people in need,
Did not offer a helping hand."

"O Lord, I have failed to reflect You today,
To mirror Your beauty and love,
No one saw You in me as I passed on my way
Too busy to bring them Your word.
So now, at the end of the day, I'm cast down,
For I've no worthwhile offering to bring,
But I ask Your forgiveness, in Christ's precious name,
As I offer, just these broken things."

Continued

142

Don't be discouraged, my friend, as you look
At the failures and sins of the day.
Lift your eyes to the Saviour, Who died on the cross
And has risen to show us His way.
He gathered the pieces of broken bread
He had blest that day by the sea.
Nothing is wasted, when offered to Him,
Broken pieces though they may be.

The Rainbow and the Cross

Genesis 8:9

The rainbow is very special to me. As William Wordsworth
says in his poem, 'The Rainbow.'
My heart leaps up when I behold
A rainbow in the sky.

W.H. Griffith Thomas wrote:-
"While we do not always see a rainbow owing to the clouds
hiding the sun, yet if we could get above the clouds we
should see the rainbow on them. Thus, there is never rain
without a rainbow being visible, if we could only get to the
right spot to see it. But God always sees it."
Genesis 9:13, "I do set my bow in the cloud."

That Sabbath morn was cool and dry and calm.
I went to church and prayed and sang the Psalms.
The Pastor read from Genesis, God's word,
All about Noah's ark and of the flood.
He read verse one in chapter number eight,
'And God remembered Noah,' was his text.
When Noah left the ark he thought of God.
We're told, he built an altar to the Lord.

Yes, Noah after all the storm and flood
Remembered God as on dry land he stood.
He could have been so occupied with plans
Of what he'd do, without the help of man,
To build again a life on this fresh earth.
'Twould be a whole new life, a real new birth.
So much was to be done but Noah paused,
And offered a burnt offering unto God.

Continued

We're told that God was pleased with Noah's act.
It was, to Him, a fragrant sacrifice.
And there, God made a covenant with man,
That never, ever would a flood again
Destroy the earth; He made His promise so
That, in the clouds we'd see His lovely bow,
His token, set in colours in the sky.
His promise sure, He'll all our needs supply.

But, more than this God did for you and me.
He sent His only Son to Calvary.
His blood, the only sacrifice for sin
Can God accept when we return to Him.
The rainbow in the cloud, a promise sure
That seasons, day and night, will still endure
While earth remains; seedtime and harvest too;
God's word: each year we see it all anew.

She Worshipped Him

She Worshipped Him

Matthew 15

She came and worshipped Him
In her great need.
It seemed that Christ refused
To hear her plead,
"O, Son of David, help
My daughter's ill."
But He continued silent
To her still.
And yet she followed hard
After the Lord,
Crying her need, and waiting
On His word.

"Send her away," was the
Disciples cry.
"I'm sent to Israel,"
Was Christ's reply.
But still she worshipped Him,
And still she prayed,
"Lord, help me, help me please,"
He heard her say.
"I cannot take the bread
From Israel's child
And give it unto dogs,"
The Lord replied.

With these stern words the Lord
Seemed to withdraw
From this poor Gentile soul
Whose need He saw.
But still she worshipped Him,
And still implored,
Undaunted by the answer
Of the Lord.
"You speak the truth to me,
But dogs can eat
The crumbs that fall around

Continued

Their master's feet."

This woman's living faith,
That Christ the Lord,
Would meet her daughter's need
Had its reward.
"Your faith is great, O woman,
As you will,
Your child is cured of all
That made her ill."
And so, she found, His word
Had healing power.
Her daughter was made whole
That very hour.

She worshipped Christ the Lord,
Made clear her need
Until He answered her,
Despite her creed.
And we can know His answer
To our need
When we, in humble faith,
Draw near and plead,
Our souls must follow hard
After our Lord,
And worship Him, the true
And Living Word.

Time Enugh

II Corinthains 6:2

There was a dream told, many years ago,
The dreamer? But his name I do not know:
Of how he dreamed of Satan on his throne,
His evil spirits gathered, all unknown,
A-waiting his commands, set to obey
His wily words, his wicked, sinful ways,
When suddenly, he asked, midst evil mirth,
"Who will go forth to ruin souls on earth?"

One bright young devil answered first, "I will,
I'll tell them there's no God," his voice was shrill.
"That will not do," said Satan gloomily,
"Men know there is a God to face some day.
They may deny it now, stifle the thought,
But when in sickness or to death they're brought,
Then deep within their hearts they know there's One.
That story will not lead them unto ruin."

Again from Satan came that question, stark,
"Who will go forth to ruin souls on earth?"
"I will," a second evil one replied.
"I'll tell them God exists," he said with pride,
"But that they're much too bad to come to Him."
"No, that won't do; their evil deeds, their sin,
Drives them to God. They've only got to read
His Holy Word to know He'll meet their need".

Once more the dreamer heard the question ring
Throughout the courts of darkness, "Who will bring
Ruin to the souls of men on earth?"
There was a pause and then a third stood forth.
"What will you tell them?" Satan questioned him,
"What will you do to help ruin them?"
"Oh, I'll encourage souls," his voice was slow,
"I'll tell them there's a God that they can know".

Continued

"How will that ruin them?" his master cried,
"I'll tell the truth," the wily one replied.
"I'll tell them God, in love, has given His Son
To die for them and that each soul may come
To Him Who offers him salvation from
His sin – that it is free to everyone,
It is the gift of God and not of works.
Oh, they will hear it all, I'll nothing shirk."

The evil spirit added fiendishly,
"I'll tell them that the Gospel's true," said he,
"But that there's time enough to come to God,
Tomorrow they can think about His love."
A murmur of applause passed through the court,
The Prince of Darkness, pleased by this report
Sent forth his evil spirit and today
Thousands are listening – "time enough," he says.

Only a dream? This plot was planned in Hell.
"Wait till you are older, you are strong and well,
No need just yet to give your soul to Christ,
Enjoy the pleasures offered, taste of life,
"There's time enough," is whispered in your ear
When you have heard the Gospel message clear.
'Too late,' will be the sinner's awful cry.
Eternal life is offered now, today.

The Water Pot

John 4:28

She was so tired of all her weary way.
Nothing had changed, day followed after day,
The same old journey out to Jacob's well
In the hot sun; she found it hard to tell
Which day it was, the heavy water pot
A burden never shared, no cosy talk
With friendly neighbours, always there alone,
Never a word or smile on her way home.

Then came the day she set off for the well,
Unhappy, tired, her life a living hell
Of loneliness, needing, she knew not what,
Her soul as empty as her water pot.
And there, at Jacob's well, she met the Christ
Who was the answer to her soul's great thirst.
She took the Living Water from the Lord,
Drank deeply from the cup He offered her.

This woman met the Christ at Jacob's well,
And her first action was to go and tell
Her neighbours what had happened to her soul,
How she had found new life, had been made whole,
And at the well she left her water pot,
The symbol of her earthly sinful lot.
Old things had passed away, fear, sin and shame,
She'd met the Christ, would never thirst again.

Our soul's great thirst cannot be satisfied
By the delights in which the world takes pride.
We keep on searching for the 'something more'
To fill the empty place in our heart's core.
The answer to our need is found in Christ
The Living Water, bringing us new life.
Oh leave your empty water pot of sin
And find your thirst is satisfied in Him.

My Father Cares

Psalm 139

The hedges were high on the narrow road
Which led from the village hall,
'Twas a lovely walk on a summer day
To reach my family abode,
But on winter nights, without any light,
It seemed that danger lurked
Behind every hedge and every bush,
Setting hearts beating fast with fright.

Many a journey from hall to home
Was shadowed by many fears,
And although imagined, those fears in my mind
Made me fearful of travelling alone.
Then such peace and such joy would come to my heart
When I'd find, along the way,
That my father had come to meet his child
And he'd hold my hand tight in the dark.

Many long years have passed and gone,
And with them my father too,
But I still remember the touch of his hand
When I was afraid and alone.
Now my Father in heaven watches my way
And when I'm afraid and alone,
He holds my hand and I hear Him say,
"Fear not, I am close, all the day".

"Tenderly He watches over you
Every step, every mile of the way,
As a mother watches o'er her baby
He'll be with you every hour of the day."

~ This poem came from my own experience in childhood.
We lived in the country and many nights I was terrified,
walking home from the 'Brownies.'

Poured Out

II Samuel 23:15

"Oh for a drink, a drink out of the well
Of clear, cool water there, at Bethlehem.
My strength is nearly gone, my thirst is great,
Oh for the water there, at Bethlehem's gate."

David, the king, was shut up in a cave
With many of his men, loyal and brave.
The town of Bethlehem was occupied
By Philistines, when David, worn and tired,
Uttered a cry of longing and of need,
And three strong men performed their worthy deed.

There, in the dead of night, midst all their foes
King David's loyal men crept on their toes,
And from the well at Bethlehem's guarded gate
They risked their lives to bring the king a drink.
His wish was their command and so they strove
To serve the master whom they greatly loved.

When David found out what his men had done,
The dangers they had faced to serve their king,
He poured the water out unto the Lord
And cried to him in these heart rending words,
"Be it far from me, oh my gracious God
To drink this water, for it is the blood
Of these my faithful men, loyal and true,
So here I pour it as my gift to You."

David, the king, poured out this precious gift,
This water gained at such a risk of life,
For he had learned, midst all his strife and sin
That God was his Redeemer and to Him
He owed his all; all his obedience,
All of his love and all of his allegiance.

Continued

Our mighty Lord broke through the enemy lines
As David's men broke through the Philistines,
And won for all, our access to the springs
Of Living Water – Christ our Saviour brings
Through Calvary, His answer to our thirst,
His poured-out blood – Water of Life – for us.

Disfigured For You

Isaiah 52:14

The fire spread quickly through the silent house,
The crackling sound of burning wood aroused,
From her deep sleep, a woman, beautiful
In face and form, a mother, by fear stilled
As death and danger crept on tongues of flame,
Licking the doors, cracking the window panes.
And in her room, a yard across the hall
Her daughter slept, her only child, her all.

No thought of self entered the mother's mind
As, spurred by love, she groped about to find
The bedroom door; the scorching heat and smoke
Blinding her eyes, making her cough and choke.
She reached her daughter's room, her dear child's bed,
Lifted her up and through the flames she sped
Taking them both to safety, unaware
The fire had scarred her face beyond repair.

The years rolled on, her daughter grew to look
As lovely as her mother had in youth,
But now her scarred, disfigured hands and face
Contrasted sharply with the young girl's grace.
They were good friends but neither voiced her thoughts
Of that one day when mother love had bought
Her daughter beauty, love and life,
And counted not the cost or yet the price.

They sailed, one day, upon a pleasure trip.
Many young people gathered on the ship.
Laughter and sun filled all the sunny hours,
But soon, the wind grew chill, the sun sank lower;
Her daughter sat beside a strange young man
Absorbed in one another, holding hands,
Not noticing the ship had reached the pier,
Her mother shivering in the cool, sea air.

Continued

The poor, scarred woman walked toward the seat
Where the young couple dreamed in friendship sweet,
Intending, in her love, to place a wrap
Around her daughter's shoulders where she sat.
The boy looked up and saw her standing near,
And in a voice not meant for her to hear,
Said to the girl, "That ugly woman there
With the disfigured face, do you know her?"

Her lovely daughter looked her in the eye,
"I don't know who she is," and walked away,
Leaving her mother there alone, eyes dry,
Too hurt to speak, too wounded sore to cry.
Love to the uttermost saved her from the flames,
But she denied that love, she was ashamed
Of all the ugliness, the beauty lost
To save her life but at such a dreadful cost.

Another was disfigured, beaten, killed,
Upon a wooden cross on Calvary's hill.
Bur man, to his great shame, has turned his back,
Denied the Saviour's last, great selfless act.
Love to the uttermost was graciously poured
On each of us – we read it in His word.
For He is able – He has borne the cost
To save all men unto the uttermost.

The Lost Coin

Luke 15:8-10

Anna was poor, a widow, all alone,
Her life was hard, she hadn't any sons.
None to support her, none to bring her joy,
She spent her days in seeking to employ
Her talents, so that she might keep herself.
She carried water, gathered sticks, but wealth
Was never hers, only one thing she owned,
Her precious headband of ten silver coins.

Anna had brought the headband from her home,
Her father's marriage gift, ten silver coins,
Her dowry, gathered at great sacrifice
And loved by Anna, not for its great price,
But for the treasured memories in each coin,
Her father's love with which two hearts were joined.
She'd kept this precious gift through all these years,
Through all the joys, the sorrows and the tears.

One morning Anna lifted her headband
To wear it to a wedding, close at hand.
She placed it on her head, then counted fast,
One coin was missing, Anna was aghast,
Where had she lost it? What was she to do?
Her precious ornament! Her panic grew,
She searched in cupboards, underneath the bed,
She swept the floor, "God help me, please," she prayed.

The light was waning, darkness soon came down,
Still Anna had not found her precious coin.
Her grief was very great, her tears flowed fast,
She lit her only candle and it cast
Its feeble light into the gloom around,
And then she saw it, shining on the ground,
Caught in a crevice almost at her feet.
Her precious coin was found, her band complete.

Continued

A thankful Anna hurried to the feast
Her worries gone, she joined the wedding guests.
"Rejoice with me, rejoice with me," she cried
And showed her lovely ornament with pride.
"I thought my precious headband was quite spoiled.
I lost one of my treasured coins and toiled
All day to find where it had gone.
Rejoice with me, my friends, I found my coin."

Our Saviour came to seek and save the lost
By dying for us on a cruel cross.
For man has wandered far away from God
And all are lost, we read it in His word.
Our Father God's great love is shown to man,
The breadth and depth and length and height has spanned
In Christ, the gulf that's fixed by sin,
'Til man repents and finds new life in Him.

~ Likewise, I say unto you, there is joy in the presence of
the angels of God over one sinner that repenteth.

The Hands of Jesus

Luke 24:40

"He's got the whole world in His hands," men often sing.
Those hands belong to Christ, the King of Kings.
Sharp nails were driven through them on a cross,
To hold Him while He suffered there for us.
God manifest in flesh, His human hands
Outstretched to every man in every land.
He has the whole world in His hands, 'tis true,
The King of Kings is holding on to you.

His hands were tiny hands when He was born
To Mary, on that cold December morn.
She must have kissed them as all mothers do,
Examined every fingernail and knew
Each crease and dimple of those baby hands,
As Christ the King lay, wrapped in swaddling bands.
The angels bid the shepherds go and see
Those hands which would be fastened to a tree.

His tiny hands grew strong until, at last,
A carpenter's fine tools within their grasp
He fashioned chairs and tables, mended ploughs,
Hewed timber into beauty, turning now
The hands which fashioned stars to toiling hands;
His workmanship makes perfect sinful man
That he might honour, glorify and praise
God's holy name those toiling hands were raised.

The tender hands of Christ were often laid
In love upon the little children's heads.
And those who came for healing to Him found
Completeness in His touch and many, bound
By sin, received forgiveness and new life
And freedom from the hands of Jesus Christ.
Those tender hands have still their ancient power
To heal, forgive and keep us hour by hour.

Continued

The hands of Christ our Lord are cleansing hands,
Saving and cleansing us from sin's demands.
With those pure hands He laid aside His robe
And washed the dusty feet of those who would,
In a few hours, deny their Friend and Lord
And run away, by fear turned into cowards,
And leave Him there, alone, on Calvary,
Those cleansing hands nailed to that cruel tree.

The praying hands of Christ plead at God's throne
For all who call upon His precious name.
Those wounded hands, which bled for you and me,
While He hung there in dreadful agony,
Are raised in intercession for all men,
That they may all be one who come to Him.
And in those hands is deepest certainty,
A providence divine and majesty.

The hands of Christ our Saviour are secure,
For He has promised and His word is sure,
That those who love Him have eternal life,
Shall never perish in this world of strife.
And He has promised no one ever can
Snatch us out of His own pierced hands.
So, held secure, we all one day shall stand
Before our God –
Who's got the whole world in His hands.

~ Idea from Streams in the Desert Sampler by Mrs. Cowman

The Good Samaritan

Luke 10

Sarah lived all her life on Albert Street,
From a small child the neighbours that she'd meet
Were her dear friends, each ready with a hand
When needed, always having time to stand
And talk, about the weather, price of coal,
Of food, of who was sick and growing old.
All a familiar pattern but now, changed,
Neighbours had died or moved, now all was strange.

People, with coloured skins from foreign parts,
Moved into Albert Street, changing its heart,
Its sights, and sounds and smells, all of them new
Made Sarah insecure; this feeling grew
As, day by day, she left her home to walk
Along her street, but, unfamiliar talk,
Strange words, assailed her ears,
She felt afraid but could not voice her fears.

Her daughter lived a long bus ride away
And Sarah tried to visit her each day
To help take care of Mark, her dear grandson,
Her fears forgotten when she left her home.
Those foreigners, Asians from Pakistan,
With their queer ways she could not understand,
But every night she said 'goodbye' to Mark
And hurried home before it got too dark.

One day she was delayed and night had come
Before she got the bus to take her home.
The street seemed shadowed, many lights were out
As Sarah hurried on, hearing the shouts
Of laughter through closed doors, music and noise,
Which drowned the footsteps of two vicious boys
Who suddenly appeared out of the night.
"Give us your handbag, Missus, and keep quiet!"

Continued

Poor Sarah could not quite believe her ears,
"Now, don't be daft," she said, amidst her tears
"Get yourselves home to bed and let me be."
But she was punched and pushed, she could not see,
Her bag was snatched and she fell to the ground,
"Help me," she cried but no one was around,
So there she lay, bleeding and bruised, clothes torn,
She could not move – all she could was groan.

Sarah despaired of help coming her way,
She could not raise her head, could only pray,
"Lord Jesus, help me," then footsteps came near;
A man across the street paused, thought, 'that's queer'
But did not stop, Sarah was left alone,
Her mouth so sore all she could do was moan.
Two older women stopped, "Just look, she's drunk,
That shows you to what depths this street has sunk,"
And on they went without a second thought
For Sarah, lying there frightened, distraught.

But help was close at hand, a car drew up,
An anxious face bent over hers, "Tut, tut
Poor lady, you're in much, much trouble,"
Sarah could only stare and groan and gurgle.
It was the man next door from Pakistan
Who gently lifted her and helped her stand,
He put her in his car, wrapped in a rug,
And drove her to the nearest casualty ward.

Sarah was overwhelmed by all his care.
Next day a card arrived with lovely flowers,
'Best wishes, get well soon', the message said.
Sarah could not believe the words she read,
She thought of all the times she'd turned away
Without a word, when he had said, 'good-day.'
She felt ashamed, this man from Pakistan
Had shown her love – a Good Samaritan.

Continued

164

This story of the Good Samaritan
Was told by Jesus when a bright young man
Asked Him, one day, "Who is my neighbour, Lord?"
Christ answered him in short and simple words,
"Go, do thou likewise." This command still rings
Down through the years; to all of us it brings
Its challenge in our selfish, busy lives.
Who is my neighbour? Go and do likewise.

The first commandment says that you shall love
With all your heart and soul the Lord your God,
And after that your neighbour as yourself.
But we love Him because He first loved us.
Christ gave His life upon that cruel cross
To save all men from sin and death and loss.
He calls us all to love and follow Him,
Then we can all be Good Samaritans.

~ I read the story, from which I wrote this poem,
in Willowfield Parish Church Magazine

The Trial

I dreamed, one night, that in a court I stood
Before a judge, in wig and gown and hood,
The room was full of people come to stare,
Curious to know why I was standing there.
I looked around and thought that I could see
Familiar faces, all were watching me,
And then, the judge read out, from a long list
The charge … 'You're not a follower of Christ.'

There, in my dream, I heard the judge's words,
"You are accused of not following the Lord,
You in the dock there, what have you to say,
How do you plead, not guilty, yea or nay?"
I heard my trembling words, "Not guilty, sir,"
And all around the court there was a stir.
"What proof have you to bring, what's your defence?
Now call your witnesses with evidence."

I looked into the faces crowding round
And then a neighbour's frowning face I found.
I called her to the box, "Now, tell the court,"
She'll give them proof I follow Christ, I thought.
"It is commanded that you love," she said,
"Your neighbour as yourself – or so I've read,
This woman in the dock has passed by me
Without a word or smile – no Christian, she."

Again I looked around among the crowd.
A coloured child came forward, crying loud.
"I was an hungered but no bread you gave,
You watched me on TV, thought you would save
A pound or two, to send to Africa,
To feed and clothe that little child you saw
Starving, in need, but you 'forgot' somehow,
'Suffer the children' has no meaning now."

Continued

I looked, in panic, at the staring crowd
And saw my family sitting with heads bowed,
And to my witness stand I called my son,
Certain he'd tell of the good things I'd done.
"But, Mum," he said, "you always talk of love,
But you are often cross; impatient words
Are on your tongue, you shout at us,
Your actions hurt, you're always in a fuss."

I stood there in that dock before that crowd,
I could not look at them, my head was bowed
In guilt and shame, not one of them could prove
I served the Lord – I did not show His love
To neighbours, family, others in their need.
'I' was important to myself, indeed
My outward actions showed no inward grace.
The judge pronounced – I had not proved my case.

I wakened from my dream, a sense of guilt
Stayed with me through the night, I felt
Confused, afraid, where was my precious Lord?
I rose up from my bed, I read His word,
And then I prayed, "I will confess to You
My God, my lack of love; make me anew
And mould me in Your image; let me be
So like my Lord that He'll be seen in me."

Who Killed the Duck

On Tommy's birthday he received a lot
Of lovely presents, one, a catapult,
His father warned him, time and time again,
As he played with it all around the farm.
Tommy enjoyed himself and he became
Quite a good shot, when he took time to aim.

On Tommy's father's farm lived four prize ducks,
The winners of a dozen silver cups,
Dear to his father's heart were those fine birds
And Tommy often heard his warning words,
"Be careful of those ducks, don't do them harm,"
As he viewed Tommy's present with alarm.

One sunny afternoon Tommy went out
To play around with his new catapult.
The four prize ducks were swimming in the pond,
Dipping for food, tails in the air, heads down.
Those tails were his undoing, he took aim,
But all went wrong with Tommy's little game.

One of the ducks had, just then, raised its head,
Tom's shot was good, one of the ducks was dead!
It's lifeless body floated on the pond,
One of those ducks of which his dad was fond!
What would he do, the duck must not be found?
He dug a hole and hid it in the ground.

Tom's father could not solve the mystery,
And Tom hoped it would soon be history.
Next morning he went whistling to the door,
His sister called him, "Tommy, wash that floor."
He looked amazed, "I'll not, that's your hard luck."
She smiled at him and said, "Who killed the duck?"

Continued

168

From then on poor Tom's life was one hard round.
He washed and scrubbed and polished to the sound
Of, "Tom, who killed the duck, who killed the duck?"
He could not stand it, he felt he was stuck
In a bad dream, weighed down by guilt
And all because he'd fired that catapult.

Tommy was losing sleep, what could he do?
His life was not worth living and he grew
More and more guilty as the days passed by.
He could not go on living such a lie.
Grabbing his catapult he went to seek
His dad, heart thumping, knees knocking, legs weak.

Tom's father listened as his son confessed
That he had killed the duck, tho' he had guessed
From Tommy's manner many days before
That he was guilty; Tommy's heart was sore,
But then his father took him in his arms,
"You are forgiven, my son, do no more harm."

Next morning Tommy whistled once again,
His sister made her threats but all in vain,
"Dad knows I killed the duck, I have confessed,"
And off he ran, no longer fear oppressed.
He'd told his father, he was free from guilt,
He'd be more careful with his catapult.

This parable of Tom and of the duck
Teaches a lesson while amusing us.
For we, like Tom, have tried to hide our sin,
But we are bound with guilt, we can't begin
To be set free 'til we ask pardon from
Our Father God through Christ His Precious Son.

Jarius' Daughter

Luke 8:41-54

Jairus' little girl, aged twelve, was dying,
The doctors could not tell him what was wrong,
They did not offer any hope of healing
For this young child who had been fit and strong.
Her mother would not leave her daughter's bedside,
The house was filled with sadness and despair
This lovely child was dear to all the family,
Their hearts were sick with hopelessness and fear.

Jairus was a leader in the temple,
Respected by the rulers and his friends.
But now, his heart was breaking with this sorrow,
Yet he believed God would some guidance send,
He'd prayed throughout the long night for an answer,
Then came a servant with most welcome news,
Jesus of Nazareth, teacher, prophet, healer,
Had crossed the lake with His small band of Jews.

Jairus had heard the rumours about Jesus
How He could heal the sick, the blind, the lame.
Many believed He was the promised Saviour
Jairus' faith reached out in the midst of pain.
Was Jesus Christ God's answer to their problem?
Would Jesus heal their precious, little girl?
He'd go and ask Him, now, this very moment,
"Lord, come and heal our child, Lord, make her well."

Jairus pushed through the gathered crowds with Jesus,
Who suddenly stood still along the way.
"Someone has touched Me, someone seeking healing,
Some person in the crowd is healed today."
Poor Jairus; anxious to keep moving,
Joined the disciples as they looked around,
"Many have touched You Jesus, pressed against You,"
A trembling woman knelt upon the ground.

Continued

The Saviour listened to the stammered story,
Twelve years of sickness, loneliness and pain.
"My daughter, go in peace, your faith has healed you",
Then Jairus heard his servant call his name.
"There is no point in troubling Jesus further,
Your little daughter is already dead."
The dreadful words were like a blow to Jairus,
But Jesus spoke, "Fear not, trust Me," He said.

With Peter, James and John they hurried onward,
Around the house people began to weep,
"Why all this wailing, why all this commotion?
The little maiden is not dead, she sleeps."
The crowd laughed scornfully at Jesus' statement,
But, asking them to leave He took her hand.
"Get up, my girl", He lovingly commanded.
The little girl jumped up and walked around.

Her parents overjoyed and full of wonder,
At Jesus' word gave her some food to eat.
He asked them not to broadcast what had happened,
Then left that home where death had known defeat.
Jairus' faith was tested to the utmost,
That agonising wait, his daughter's death.
But Jesus filled his soul with hope and comfort,
Victorious life and joy rewarded faith.

In Jesus Christ we have the only answer
To life and death, disease and pain and strife.
A woman's hand reached out and touched the Saviour,
His hands reached out and gave a child new life.
Those outstretched hands are marked with cruel nail prints,
They're reaching out to save us from our sin.
Stretch out your hand to Jesus Christ the Saviour,
He'll lift you up, you'll find new life in Him.

That Day

John 11

That day will live forever in my mind.
Each time I look at Lazarus I find
My memory paints again those scenes now past;
The days of dreadful suffering and at last
His death, while we, my sister and myself,
Waited despairing, having sent for help,
Not understanding why our dearest Friend,
Our Lord, was silent; why He did not send
Some word of comfort to us in our grief,
Or come Himself, His presence our release
From all the pain and sorrow of our loss,
But then, we did not know about the cross.

The three of us had lived in Bethany
All of our lives, a happy family.
Our brother Lazarus was dear to us,
Filling our home with laughter, friends and fuss.
Mary enjoyed it all and joined the fun;
But I held back, I was the eldest one,
And, I confess, my patience, often strained
To breaking point, was lost, then I'd complain,
But through it all our lives were lit by love
For one another and for God above.
We looked for the fulfilling of His word,
The promised Christ, in Whom our hopes were stored.

Jesus of Nazareth had become our Friend.
Lazarus had met Him first and then
Had brought Him to our home in Bethany,
Where Jesus found renewal in our midst
And many of His followers came to hear His word.
My sister Mary always called Him Lord,
She seemed to understand, much more than I,
That He was special, but I always tried
To make our home a quiet resting place
For Him, when Lazarus would come with haste
To tell us He was on His way again. Continued

Such joy was ours, but later came the pain.

It happened suddenly, Lazarus fell ill.
We did not know how sick he was until
The doctor called us to his side,
The shock so great we both stood their and cried.
But then, we thought of Jesus, knew we could send
For Him and He would come and heal His friend,
But there was only silence and instead,
When Jesus came at last, Lazarus was dead,
Already in the tomb for four long days!
We went to meet the Lord along the way,
"If You had only come he'd be alive,
Why did You wait and let our brother die?"

Our Saviour's love reached to us in our grief.
"I am the resurrection and the life,
He that believes on Me shall never die,
Can you believe this, Martha?" and I cried,
"I do believe Thou art the Christ, the Son
Of God and what You ask, it will be done."
We went with Jesus then to Lazarus' tomb,
Where we could not control our tears and soon
The Lord wept with us in our grief,
And all those standing round, in unbelief
Listened and watched as unto God He prayed
And called our brother Lazarus from the grave.

That day our Lord changed sorrow into joy
For Mary and myself, death was destroyed.
We did not know another day would come
When Christ, Himself, would rise up from a tomb.
We had to stand and watch our Saviour die
Upon a cross, there on Mount Calvary.
But, as He raised our brother from the grave,
So God raised Jesus up to be our Head,
Our Resurrection, our Eternal Life,
Offered to all men in this world of strife.
His Spirit lives in us, He sets us free
To live our lives in Him victoriously.

Now Jesus loved Martha and her sister and Lazarus.

Were You There?

Many were there that day when Jesus died.
They stood and watched as He was crucified.
The Pharisees and priests, glad to be rid
Of this 'upstart,' Whose every word and deed
Had challenged their position and their power.
This Jesus would be dead within the hour.
He'd claimed to be Messiah, King of the Jews,
Now they relaxed, His threat to them removed.

The soldiers sat around and watched Him there.
They gambled for His clothes but did not dare
Divided His robe; thus prophecy, Psalm twenty-two
Was now fulfilled; God's word came true
Through men, whom Jesus prayed God to forgive,
While He hung there and looked at them in love.
Those men, who'd nailed Him to that cruel tree
Christ Jesus died to save, on Calvary.

Peter stood at a distance from the cross,
Ashamed of his denial, at a loss
To understand, how he, who loved his Lord
So much, in the priest's hall denied that love
And turned away and left Him there alone.
He, who'd protested loyalty, had sworn
Never to leave Him, he had run away
And left his Lord to die on Calvary.

Mary, His mother, watched as her Son died,
Her heart so full of pain she could not hide
The tears and sobs which shook her feeble form.
Fond memories filled her mind; the day that He was born,
The visit to the temple in Jerusalem.
She'd watched Him grow from boy to man
And draw the crowds of needy to His side,
But now, her Son hung dying, crucified.

Continued

John stood with Mary as the Saviour died,
His arm around her shoulders as he tried
To bring some comfort to her in her pain.
He heard the loving words from his dear Friend,
"She is your mother, take her to your home."
And, to His mother, "John will be your son".
The love of Christ shone from that dreadful cross
As they consoled each other in their loss.

The Roman soldier had seen many die
That awful death there on Mount Calvary
But none had died as this man here today.
"Father, forgive them," he had heard Him pray.
He'd heard His words of love to the dying thief,
He'd heard Him speak to His mother in her grief.
The soldier's heart was touched by the dying Lord,
"Truly," he said, "this is the Son of God."

Were you there when they crucified the Lord?
Did you stand there, and listen to His words?
Did you hear His, 'Father, forgive their sins'?
Did you join those who jeered and laughed at Him?
Did you look up and see His nail-pierced hands,
His wounded side, head crowned with those awful thorns?
Did you see the love which shone from those pain-filled
eyes
And hear His, 'It is finished,' as He died?
His love poured out to save us all from sin,
Come to the cross, you'll find new life in Him.

Matthew

Matthew 9:9-13, 28:18-20

"And lo I'm with you all the days," Christ said,
"Even unto the very end." He laid
His pen upon the page and closed His eyes.
How weary he was now, how very old.
The years had gone just as a tale that's told,
But joy and peace remained in Matthew's heart
As they had filled it from the very start,
The day the Lord had called him from his desk
And then gone home with Matthew as his Guest.

Memory took over then in Matthew's mind.
As tax-collector in Capernaum
He'd had few friends, was hated by the Jews
Because he worked for Rome, and many knew
He wasn't honest, took more than was due,
And lined his pockets, taking from the poor,
His only friends were sinners, like himself,
Collaborators, hated for their wealth,
And so, his life was lonely, lacking love -
Until the day he met the Son of God.

Matthew had heard the rumours of the Christ
Who'd roused such anger in the Jewish priests,
Performing miracles in Galilee;
The paralysed made whole, the blind made see,
The lame was made to walk, his sins forgiven,
And Matthew longed to meet this Friend of men
Who seemed to be the answer to his need -
His need to be set free from guilt and greed.
Surely this Man called Christ could make him whole,
Could take the darkness from his weary soul.

Then Jesus came one day and Matthew met
The Son of God, there, on Capernaum street.
"Come, follow Me," the Saviour said to him,
And Matthew rose, left all, his job, his sin
And followed the Lord Jesus in the way.

He opened up his home that very day *Continued*
And with the Saviour as his honoured Guest
He gave a feast that all might meet the Christ,
The publicans and sinners whom he knew,
He wanted them to have this new life too.

Matthew remembered clearly how the Jews,
The Pharisees and Scribes, received the news
That Jesus was a friend to men like him,
Would sit and eat a meal with publicans;
And Jesus' answer – that He came to call
The sinner, not the righteous, to be whole.
Matthew remembered all the Lord had said
And done, in those short years before He paid
The price for sin, by dying on the cross
To save all men from sin and death and loss.

Matthew leaned wearily against his chair,
Recalling, once again, the real nightmare
Of the disciples when their Lord had gone,
And their great joy, when, in the early morn
The Lord appeared to them in Galilee,
And said, "All power is given unto Me,
Go ye and teach all nations, baptise them
In God the Father, Son, and Spirit's name,
And lo, I'm with you always, with all men.
I'll be with you", He said, "unto the end."

The Upper Room

Luke 22, John 13

I've often wondered why the Lord chose me.
I wasn't one of the close band, you see.
In fact, I'd only come to love Him late,
I'd heard Him teaching at the temple gate
One day, His words just seemed to be for me,
He offered me forgiveness, set me free
From all the sins that burdened my sore heart.
He changed my life, He gave me a new start.
And every day my love for Him has grown
And filled me with a joy 'till now unknown.

Jerusalem was my home all of my life,
I lived there with my children and my wife.
We were good Jews, we tried to keep the law,
Observed the holy days and always saw
That all of God's commandments were obeyed,
But when Christ Jesus spoke to me that day
I understood, at last, what God's love meant
And that this Man, called Jesus, had been sent
To bring to all, forgiveness for our sin,
When we repent and put our trust in Him.

Jerusalem was packed with pilgrim Jews.
The feast of Passover was nearly due
When Jesus came to visit in our home
And asked me to reserve our upper room
That He might keep the feast with His close friends
In private – no one was to know, for men,
Religious leaders, sought to have Him killed
Because He spoke of God, against their will,
As Father and Himself as God's own Son,
Messiah, promised from of old, the Holy One.

Continued

Jesus and I agreed a secret sign;
His friends would follow, at a certain time,
A man, whom they would notice in the street,
Carrying a water-pot and then, they'd greet
Me with the words, "Where is the guestchamber?"
"The Master says, that we may now prepare
The feast of the Passover He wants to share
With His disciples." – All was set with care,
But I was ill at ease, I felt afraid,
Something was wrong – Jesus would be betrayed.

Christ washed the feet of all His friends, that night,
He broke the bread that all might have a bite.
"My body broken for you all," He said,
And then, they shared the cup, "I am betrayed
By one who shares with us." All of them gasped,
"Who is it? Is it I?" were questions asked,
And Judas, looking guilty, left the room.
I saw it all and knew that, very soon,
My friend would die – this Man who'd saved my soul,
Had set me free from sin and made me whole.

The Lord has chosen you, as He chose me,
He'll enter every life and set us free.
He asks for the guest chamber of our hearts
That He might share our lives in every part.
His body, broken for us all, He shares,
His blood poured out for all in love and care.
Give Him that upper room, that guestchamber,
Give Him the right He has to enter there,
He knocks and asks for entrance to our souls,
That He may sup with us and make us whole.

The Boat

Luke 19:10

It sat in the front window of the shop,
Graceful, blue hull and pure, white sails on top,
The loveliest boat that John had ever seen,
Carved out of wood, its lines were long and clean,
T'would sail upright and fast upon the lake;
So John determined, there and then, to take
His savings from his box to buy this boat,
Among his friends 'twould be the best afloat.

The little boy marched in and asked the cost
Of that fine boat, he came out looking lost.
His pocket money would not ever buy
The lovely boat, poor John tried not to cry.
He stared at it again, yes, he could make
A boat as fine to sail upon the lake.
He gathered wood and tools and drew his plans,
Anxious to hold his boat between his hands.

John cut and carved and polished, 'till at last
His boat took shape, white sails upon her mast,
Blue painted hull and red flag flying free.
He took her to the lake, so proud to see
How upright, fast and gracefully she skimmed
Over the water; soon his joy was dimmed,
His boat had sailed far, far beyond his reach
And she was lost upon some distant beach.

John's heart was broken when he lost his boat.
He wandered home, dragging his feet and coat
And all the week was spent mourning its loss,
Nothing could take its place for it had cost
So much in time and love for John to make,
No other boat could ever take its place,
And then, one day, he passed the village shop -
There was his boat with the red flag on top!

Continued

180

Into the shop John went with eyes alight,
"That boat is mine, please can I have her back?"
But he was disappointed, he was told
He'd have to buy it, it was to be sold.
John took on every job that he could find,
Ran errands, washed cars, a paper round
Until, at last, he had the money saved
To buy the boat that he, himself had made.

John paid the price demanded for his boat,
He wrapped it carefully inside his coat
And hurried home, his face alight with joy,
"You're mine, you're doubly mine," he proudly said,
"My own hands made you but you strayed,
I lost you for a while but now, you're found,
I paid the price – to me you're doubly bound,"

Creator God has made us for His own
To glorify His name we have been born,
But we have wandered far away from Him,
We're lost, astray, in this dark world of sin.
Our Saviour came to seek and save the lost,
He paid the price for us upon the cross.
We're doubly His – He made us, we were lost,
He bought us with His Blood, He paid the cost.

For the Son of Man is come to seek and to save that which
was lost.

Abba, Father

Deuteronomy 33:27

The sun shone warmly from a clear, blue sky,
The tall trees stood on tip-toe reaching high,
The hedgerows seemed alive with insect life
And all around the fields of corn were ripe.
Along the road two figures came in sight,
A father and a child, flying a kite.

The kite rose up above the lofty trees,
Dipping and sailing on the gentle breeze,
The string was held with all the small girl's might,
The father's grasp upon his child was tight,
Laughter and fun filled all the summer air,
Father and child walked on without a care.

Then, o'er the sun, dark clouds began to form,
The wind made sweeping waves among the corn,
The tall trees seemed to sway in the rising breeze,
A rustling started high up in the leaves,
The girl held tightly to her father's hand,
As darkness seemed to creep across the land.

The dusty ground soon turned to muddy pools
As rain fell heavily, the air turned cool,
The road became a slide to little feet,
Her hands let go the kite and reached to seek
The safety of her father's caring arms,
Where she'd be sheltered, warm and safe from harm.

"Please, daddy," said the child, "please carry me,
The way is very slippery, you see."
The father scooped the child up in his arms,
"I've got you, darling, now you're safe from harm."
And on they hurried 'till they reached their home.
And found there shelter from the summer storm.

Continued

182

Our heavenly Father cares for every child
Of His, however rough the way, however wild.
And He Who cares when e'en a sparrow falls,
Will stoop to help His children when they call.
His everlasting arms are underneath,
For Abba, Father cares, in life and death.

The eternal God is thy refuge and underneath are the everlasting arms.

A Little Child Shall Lead Them

Isaiah 38:17

A little girl, in Sunday school one day,
Had listened to her teacher, heard her say,
"When you confess and put your trust in Him
God will forgive His children all their sin.
And in His word we read this lovely fact,
God has cast all our sins behind His back."

The child's young heart was touched by what was said.
She knelt, that night, beside her bed and prayed,
"Lord, I am very small but I love You,
Please take my sins as You have promised to,
Put them behind Your back so I can see
There's nothing wrong between my Lord and me."

The little girl, excited told her Mum
About the lovely thing that she had done.
"They're all behind God's back, it's in His word,
My sins are all forgiven by the Lord."
Rejoicing in the faith her child had found
She asked the question, "What if God turns round?"

The little one looked thoughtfully at her,
"I know that Jesus hears and answers prayer,
I know He loves me and forgives my sin
And God, my Father, looks at me through Him,
I've read it in His Word and it is true,
So, if God turns around, His back turns too."

All Things New

Revelation 21:5

The garden was ablaze with tulips, crowds
Of lofty blooms of colour standing proud,
Flaunting their rainbow petals in the air,
Their loveliness revealing all the care
Lavished upon them by her mother's hands,
Among the many job which made demands
Upon her time – her little daughter's needs -
Refusing discipline for naughty deeds.

The sun filled garden beckoned to the child
Whose mood was angry, temper, short and wild,
Searching for something on which she could vent
The bottled feelings of her discontent.
She snatched some scissors from a kitchen drawer
And off she went; soon every tulip flower
Had lost its head; her temper cooled, she felt
Dismayed at what she'd done – consumed with guilt.

When mother found out what the child had done
Her hurt was hidden but her peace had gone.
Anxious to understand the reason why
Her child had acted so unworthily,
She took her little daughter on her knee,
"Why did you hurt the flowers and so hurt me?"
Her little girl put both arms around her neck,
"When daddy comes, he'll put their poor heads back."

So, sometime later, tulip heads appeared,
Much stronger than the ones that had been sheared.
Father had answered, lovingly, the plea
Presented by his sorry child and we
Who've sinned can turn to One, Whose love and care
Has blotted out our sins, made us His heirs
With His own Son, restored His beauty to
Our lives and, in His love, made all things new.

G.P.C.

A cotton-picker came to love the Lord,
Enthusiastic, keen to know His word,
To go to far flung foreign lands to preach,
To do some special task, perhaps to teach.
He stood among the cotton in the fields,
Eyes scanning feathery clouds which seemed to yield
A message to his eager mind and heart,
G. P. C. he read, then gave a start,
For in the sky the guidance that he wished
Was written clearly, Samuel, "Go preach Christ."

In his excitement, Samuel downed his tools
And ran to where and old man, keeping cool,
Sat in the shade of a banana tree.
"Look, look," he cried, "the letters G. P. C.
'Go preach Christ,' the Lord has said to me."
The old man raised his head, 'till he could see
The cloudy letters, "G. P. C.," he read,
"I see the G. P. C. my dear, dear son,
To me it seems to say, 'Go pick cotton.'

Where are you placed? Where falls your daily lot?
In factory, office, school or kitchen fraught
With great dullness, day following dreary day
Where nothing changes, everything seems grey?
But we are told, in God's own precious word,
To do all heartily as to the Lord.
And God requires our faithful service where
His hand has placed us and we all must share
The gospel of the love of His dear Son,
He still says, "Go preach Christ, Go pick cotton."

How Can They Hear

How can they hear?
Their ears are deafened by their hungry cries.
Their bodies, swollen, grotesque, they try
To smile, while cameras click away
Showing their agony, a living hell of hunger,
Day by day, dying the slow death, bit by painful bit,
While we, the Western World, in luxury sit.
How can they hear?

How can they hear?
The Gospel of the love of Christ our Lord?
God's sacrifice on Calvary must be shared,
But how can people, young and old, whose ears
Are closed by suffering, hunger, fear,
Hear of His love unless they see it shown
By us, who claim allegiance to His throne?
How can they hear?

How can they hear?
In Ethiopia, Sudan, Peru,
Brazil, Bolivia, other lands too,
People are starving, poverty prevails.
The answer to their need lies in ourselves,
The giving of our money, time and love,
Our prayers, as God has given us richly from above.
Then they will hear.

Count It All Joy

James 1:2a

How can I count it joy when every breath
Is choked off by the load of grief I bear?
How can I count it joy when tears stream down,
The house is still, weeping the only sound?
How can I count it joy when joy has fled
And darkness brings no sleep upon my bed?
How can I count it joy in all this pain?

But joy in Christ remains for God remains
Whatever be the circumstance or pain,
And He is still Redeemer and His touch
Of love redeems our grief, however much,
If we will pour it all – an offering –
Of love into His hands, then He will bring
His joy in pain, His joy in suffering.

Christmas Poems

Advent

He came – God's Son – to earth at Christmastime,
Born of a Virgin – One of David's line.
Angels – a star – proclaimed His Holy birth,
Shepherds and wisemen worshipped Him on earth.
All of creation welcomed Him that morn,
Rejoicing that the Son of Man was born.

He lived until the age of thirty three.
Most of those years He worked in Galilee.
With poor and sinful men He spent His days
Showing God's love and teaching them His ways.
He made the blind to see, He healed the lame,
His only aim – to glorify God's name.

This Jesus took upon Himself our sin,
Received our punishment – that He might win
Our souls from certain death to endless life.
He faced man's hatred, bore with sin and strife
For love of man, love of the Father too,
And died on Calvary for love of you.

Soon He'll return again – a second time,
Not as a baby born of David's line –
Not as our Saviour but as Christ the Lord.
Before Him all shall bow; He'll be adored
By all who owned Him Saviour – sent from God –
But Judge to all who failed to trust His word.

No Room

Luke 2:7

I didn't know –
They hadn't booked a room. You see
My inn was packed – if only I had known that night
That God's own Son would be born soon in our cowshed –
Which lacked all comfort – heat, blankets, bed;
I might – I do not know – have turned another out
And given Him the room – but in a shed!

Oh, yes – I heaped fresh hay into a pile
And spread a ragged blanket thereupon.
I placed some more and made a little nest
In the cowstall – a lovely smile of thanks was given me –
Oh – had I gone to greater lengths that starry night
And given up my rest for Him – the Saviour of the world.
Outside – above the shed – a great star shone.

He'd left His Father's home –
I wish I'd known – left all the glory,
Took on human form – a baby born –
He laid aside His kingly rights, became a servant,
God most holy – He looked so tiny lying there
In swaddling bands – His mother kissed
His little waving hands – so tenderly –
Hands by nails torn.

I didn't stay – my inn was full you see,
And so I missed the shepherds –
Missed their tale of angels singing of the Saviour's birth;
A star to guide them to my shed where He lay in the manger.
I had failed to recognise Him, God on earth.
A wooden cowshed I'd prepared for Him
Who'd come, prepared to die for all my sin.

Continued

192

I know it now – some thirty years ago
My inn was full – I had no room
To house God's Son – now in my heart He lives.
It took some time – I was so slow to understand,
Messiah come to earth – born in my humble shed –
In wooden manger laid.
Now I believe He died for me – now I've made room for
Him.

The Shepherd's Return

Luke 2:20

We'd seen and heard it all that winter night.
A multitude of angels, shining bright
Announced, in ringing tones, a Saviour's birth,
Telling the joyful news, "God come to earth."
And we would find Him in a manger laid,
A pile of hay, the pillow for His head.
We saw the shining star – it led us on
Until we found the place where He was born.

Strange that we found the babe in such a place,
Wrapped up in swaddling clothes – no sign of lace
Or fine wool shawl – no silken gown –
But we could feel the love shed all around.
And there we knelt and worshipped Christ the King.
Light shone from Him – He lit up everything –
Our hearts, our lives were changed by this sweet babe
Born of a Virgin – in a manger laid.

We left – rejoicing – praising God above
Who, in His mercy, showed infinite love
To every man on earth – we stopped and told
All who would stand and listen, in the cold,
About the things we'd heard and seen that night;
The message brought by angels and the light
Of the great star that guided from above
And led us to such joy and peace and love.

Many rejoiced with us, many believed
And joined in praising God – we all received
The truth into our souls – that God had come –
As He had promised – in His much loved Son –
To live His life in all who'd give Him room.
This was Messiah come to earth and soon –
A few short years – men would Him crucify
And stand beneath His cross and watch Him die.

Herod

Matthew 2:1-8

The first I heard about this new born King
Was, when my servants asked if they could bring
Into my presence, three men from afar,
Looking for One, Who, heralded by a star,
Was to be King – King of the Jews He'd be!
Could He become the King instead of me?

I met these Magi from the east, who said
A child was born and they'd be led
Here, to my palace in Jerusalem,
Seeking a baby Prince – to worship Him!
Disturbed, I called the teachers and the priests;
Could this be true? What did the prophets teach?

Micah, the prophet, had written that a King
Would come to earth – be born in Bethlehem.
I called the three wise men and questioned them
About the star – sent them to Bethlehem
And charged them to return when He'd been found.
Could it be so – was I to lose my throne?

They did not come – they dared to disobey!
But I made sure – there was no other way –
That He was dead by killing all the males
Around two years of age – I could not fail!
My throne is safe, the threat to it removed!
And yet –
Could it be true – a new King of the Jews?

His Name

Matthew 1:21

"Jesus, will be His name," the angel said,
"He will be great, He'll reign in David's stead,
And He will be the Saviour from all sin,
All people will be saved who trust in Him."
This Word became the Son of God on earth,
Born of a woman, but of holy birth.

"What will we call the baby?" parents ask.
To choose a name becomes a lovely task.
A boy or girl – a Peter, John or Jane,
Sara or David – so much in a name.
Mary and Joseph did not have a choice,
They heard the message, they obeyed the Voice.

Perhaps in Nazareth, when work was done,
Mary would talk about the little One.
"If He was yours what name would you give Him?"
Joseph might answer, "He'd be Abraham,
Father of all the nations, Friend of God,
But Jesus means all that – He will be Lord."

"What name would you have given Him for life?"
Joseph might ask Mary, his dear wife.
"Oh, I'd have called Him Moses", Mary said,
"A prince and a commander – made to lead
His people out of slavery and death
Into a promised land of peace and wealth,
There to obey and serve our Father, God,
But Jesus means all that – Leader and Lord."

"Perhaps we might have called Him Solomon,
For wisdom and truth will mark the Holy One.
As David's greater Son He will be known,
As Son of God He'll occupy the throne
Of heaven – before Him all shall fall.
His name is Jesus – Leader and Lord, King over all."

He Understands

'Joy to the world,' praise rings out once again,
'The Lord is King,' we hear the sweet refrain,
Christmas has come with tinsel, fir trees, snow,
Turkey and pudding, presents tied with bows.
Families and friends to celebrate Christ's birth
Choirs sweetly singing, 'Peace to men on earth'
Homes filled with grown ups, lots of girls and boys
Loved ones together in fellowship and joy.

But, not in every home does such joy reign.
Many are filled with sorrow, grief and pain.
The joy of Christmas makes them more aware
That, at the table, stands an empty chair.
And other empty hearts are filled with fears
And Christmastime, for them, brings only tears,
Many sad hearts and empty places – pain –
Christmas will never be the same again.

Where is the comfort of a mother's arm –
A father's presence guarding the home from harm?
Where is the humour of a teenage son,
A daughter's love, a grandchild in the home?
But God our Father knows the pain you bear
At Christmastime, Christ came your grief to share,
God's only Son, Who stands at God's right hand,
He knows your loss, your grief, God understands.

Too Fast

Slow down, you're going to fast,
Sit still, and let it all pass.
What if there are only twenty days more
For presents to buy and goodies to store!
Stop and consider and lift up your thoughts
To the Saviour of men, Whose birthday has brought
Joy to the world and salvation from sin.

So open your heart and let Him come in.
It's countdown to Christmas. What can you buy
For Grandma and Grandpa and Great Aunt Sophia,
For David and Sara and next door's wee Ted?
Round and around go the thoughts in your head.
Slow down for a while, you're going too fast,
Stop and sit still and let it all pass.
Lift up your heart to Jesus Who came
At this Christmastime to be Saviour of men.

He had no room in which to be born,
Only a stable, on that winter morn.
He had no boat to sail on the lake,
No money for taxes to pay to the state,
No pillow on which to lay His dear head
While foxes had holes and birds, nests for their beds.
Our Saviour was homeless, with nothing to give
But His life for us – so – slow down, and live.

The Christmas Story

My first poem written 1947

Mary was only a peasant girl
Born in a humble home,
But an angel appeared to her
And unfolded the plan God had for the world.

"Thou has been chosen of God, Mary
To bring forth the Prince of Peace."
"If it be His command," she softly replied,
"I will obey His wish."

Out on the hillside tending their sheep
The shepherds saw a star,
And wise men journeyed to Bethlehem
With presents of gold and myrrh.

They looked in the palace of Herod the King
And were told He was not there.
They tried in the inn, but because of the crowd
He was found in a stable bare.

There, Mary rocked the babe in her arms
And silently prayed to God.
While shepherds and wise men worshipped the Child
Who was born to save the world.

But the world was still waiting and watching
For the King whom the prophets foretold,
While He lay and cooed in His mother's arms,
And she called Him the Lamb of God.

The Visit of the Wise Men

Matthew 2:1-12

There was something about that baby
Lying there in the stable hay,
The cows and the sheep stood watching
As the shepherds knelt to pray.
Mary, His mother, and Joseph
Sat close by the manger stall,
We could sense the awe and the worship
And the love in the hearts of all.

We had travelled from far to see Him,
We had followed the star in the east.
We enquired of Him from King Herod
He'd be here in a palace at least.
Why was He born in a stable
In the cold back yard of an inn?
Was there no bed but a manger
For this Child who was born a King?

We knelt on the earth floor in worship
And offered our gifts to Him there,
We spread them, in love, before Him,
The frankincense, gold and myrrh.
We knew that this Child was holy,
God's Son born to live among men
That their sins might be forgiven.
But how, or where, or when?

As we turned to leave the stable
The light from the star shone within.
And it seemed to light up the manger
And it seemed to light up Him.
We looked back as we left the stable,
And each felt a sense of loss,

Continued

200

For the light had cast a dark shadow
'Twas the shadow of a cross.

~ The last verse of this poem surprised me; it just seemed to
write itself, but the shadow of the cross lies over every event
of the Christmas story as the joy and hope of the resurrection lies over the reality of the cross.

The Fir Tree

The fir tree stood by the pulpit steps.
It was Christmas Eve and the whole world slept.
He looked very fine standing straight and tall,
Covered with tinsel and silver balls.
Each green branch held a candle light
Which tomorrow would shine out clear and bright.

The fir tree was waiting for Christmas morn.
The day that the baby Jesus was born.
The church would be full for His birthday,
The people would gather to sing and pray
And bring their gifts to hang on the tree.
He was waiting to see what those gifts would be.

For he knew all about the little Christ child
Born in Bethlehem so gentle and mild.
He knew He was born to die on a tree
Because of man's sin, die to set man free
And that all that Christ wanted right from the start
Was the gift of man's love, the gift of his heart.

The church was crowded with old and young,
Prayers were said and carols were sung.
The story of Christmas was read once again,
And the children admired the nativity scene.
The little fir tree had his candles all lit
As he stood in the corner awaiting their gifts.

The children brought chocolates and sweets and balls,
Games and puzzles, toys large and small,
Train sets and lorries and bundles of books,
Food parcels, flowers and baskets of fruit.
The fir tree looked at the gifts where they lay,
But there wasn't a heart for Jesus' birthday.

Continued

202

The service was finished, the people gone home
To their turkey and pudding; the tree was alone
When a small boy, in rags, feet bare on the tiles,
Face stained with tears, crept up the aisle.
He knelt on the floor before the fir tree,
Eyes filled with wonder at what he could see.

"You're a beautiful tree," said the little boy,
"And I wanted to bring a beautiful toy,
But I hadn't a book or a toy to bring
On this Christmas day to the baby King,
So I've come to give Him all that I've got.
I'll give to the Christ child the gift of my heart."

~ The tree is the central feature of the Christmas decorations in our homes and in many of our churches. When thinking of a poem for this season which would express the gospel story in a 'new' way I hit on this idea. I hope it appeals to you.

The Shepherd Boy

I was helping my father and brothers that night
To look after the lambs and the sheep,
When a lovely, big star shone out, clear and bright,
And awakened me out of my sleep.
As I stared at the star, feeling very afraid,
An angel appeared from above,
"Fear not, for I bring you a message," he said,
"Good tidings of great joy and love."

He said that a baby, the Saviour of men,
Had been born in a cattle shed.
That the strange star would guide us to Bethlehem,
Where He lay in a manger bed.
Then around us appeared a great angel throng
Singing, "Glory to God on high."
They all flew away when they'd finished their song
And the star was alone in the sky.

We went to the stable, so rough, cold and bare,
And found as the angel had said.
The beautiful baby was lying there
Cradled in hay for His bed.
I had brought Him a present, a lamb newly born,
But Mary, His mother, looked sad,
She patted my head as she looked at her Son,
And called Him the Lamb of God.

The Little Star

"But – mine is such a little light
What use am I on a dark night?"
The tiny star sighed to the moon
"What can I do, so small am I
Amid the darkness of the sky?"

The moon smiled gently at the star,
"Our God had placed us where we are
To do His will in every way.
We all must try, we must obey
Our Father God Who made us light
That we would brightly shine at night."

The little star shone happily
Down through the years until, one day,
He realised that his small light
Had grown quite strong and in the night
It made a path as bright as day
Down to the earth, a shining way.

The God of Heaven came to him.
"My strong, bright star, your light must shine
To show the world my Son is born
In Bethlehem town; you will make known
To eastern kings the stable bare,
And Christ the King who's lying there."

Our God has placed us where He will,
In corner small or highest hill.
But we must always let our light
Shine brightly in the darkest night.
Our light is Christ, Who died to bring
Light, in the darkness of our sin.

Jesus bids us shine
With a clear, pure light.
Like a little candle
Burning in the night.
In this world of darkness   *Continued*

So we must shine,
You in your small corner
And I in mine.
~ Susan Warner

The Spaceman's Christmas

'Twas Christmas when the spaceman came to earth,
The world was celebrating Jesus' birth.
He parked his spaceship right outside the town
And then set off across the snowy ground
Towards the busy shops, the lighted streets,
The pushing crowds, with sore and weary feet,
Searching for food, for presents, Christmas cards;
The spaceman stood bewildered, looking towards
A great, tall tree covered in fairy lights
Balloons and shining tinsel, making bright
The ground beneath, where stood a man in red
With long, white beard and cap upon his head.
He did not know what it was all about
And so he was determined to find out.

The little spaceman stopped a passing man,
Arms filled with bundles, "Tell me, if you can
What mean these lights, this hurry all around,
These crowds of people hither and thither bound.
Why that great, shining tree with all the lights,
The man in red, what's going on tonight?"
"Where have you been?" he asked, "It's Christmas Eve."
The spaceman looked in wonder at the scene,
"Christmas," he echoed, "what does Christmas mean?
I've come from space, I do not understand,
Please explain Christmas to me if you can."
The stranger led the spaceman to a seat
From where they watched the people in the street.

"Well," said the man, "at Christmas time on earth
We celebrate the baby Jesus' birth.
He is God's Son, His name Emmanuel.
Born in a stable bare, in Bethlehem.
An angel host proclaimed that He was born,
And shepherds worshipped, in that early morn,
The Baby sent to save men from their sin.
And so, we celebrate and worship Him."
The little spaceman sat and looked around
At all the shops, the lighted tree, the town   *Continued*

207

So full of noisy people, pushing crowds,
Street vendors calling custom, voices loud.
He turned back to his guide and sadly asked,
"I wonder where Christ is in your Christmas?"

Never Over

"I'm so glad that's over for another year."
This is a phrase we very often hear
When all the Christmas fun has been and gone,
The crackers have been pulled, the puddings done,
The turkey bones are soup, we're tied of cake
It's time to throw the holly out and take
The garlands down, the mistletoe is dead,
Christmas is finished, the sales begin instead.

Christmas is at an end. Can this be true?
We've spent our time and money on a few
Close friends, our families and ourselves.
Unwelcome gifts are pushed to the back of shelves.
We feel let down, depressed, a sense of loss.
Completely unexplained, takes hold of us,
Is this what Christmas time is all about,
This let down feeling, this unrest and doubt?

Is Christmas time an end or a beginning
For you, my friend? Is Jesus Christ your King?
Or are you glad the festive time is only
A once year affair, and months and days
Will come and go before you think again
Of Christmas? but, peace and goodwill to men
Is not the end; it's never, ever over,
For unto us I born, this day, a Saviour.

Christmas is not the end but the beginning.
The birthday of our Lord, our heavenly King.
God manifest in flesh for our redemption.
Salvation comes to us through faith in Him.
Down to a manger bed He came from glory,
The Word made flesh; we know the Christmas story,
Our Lord became a babe in Bethlehem,
New hope, a new beginning for all men.

~ In Share My Pleasant Stones by Eugenia Price, the reading for December 26 game me the idea for this poem. She writes: "There is no reason at all why Christians should be 'let down' on the day after Christmas. If we are, it is because we have allowed the holy day to become merely a holiday. We have centred our attention around gifts and family and décor. It is no wonder we are 'let down!' ... Men and women everywhere (even Christians) sigh and say they are glad it's all over for another year ... but it isn't over ... it's just beginning! ... Christmas is forever and ever because He Himself is the end."

Mary

Luke 1:2

It's quiet here in Nazareth, tonight,
As I sit, dreaming, in the evening light.
I can recall those vivid scenes at will,
My home, Joseph, the angel Gabriel,
The kind innkeeper there in Bethlehem,
The shepherd's visit, and the strange wise men.

Joseph and I had been engaged a year.
Our wedding day was drawing very near.
I'd been quite busy, getting all prepared,
That day the angel Gabriel appeared.
At first, I did not know that it was he,
Could not believe this message was for me.

"Mary, fear not, you are God's chosen one,
You'll be the mother of His only Son,
Through Whom men will be saved from all their sin.
Jesus, will be His name and He'll be King."
My cousin too, he said, would have a son,
And she was old – God's gracious will was done.

Gabriel's message from Almighty God
Had come to me, it left me overawed.
But, all my life, I'd felt God near to me,
And, though I could not see how this could be,
I answered Gabriel, "I serve the Lord,
Be it to me according to thy word."

Nothing was easy after that strange day.
Joseph and I were married straight away.
The angel had prepared him, in a trance.
The village people gossiped, looked askance.
But God's great plan took us away from them,
We found we'd have to go to Bethlehem.

The government required that men return
To their home town to sign the census form. *Continued*

We'd have to hurry there and find a room
Where God's own Son, Messiah, could be born.
I could not walk that long and dusty way,
So Joseph bought a donkey, small and grey.

That little donkey plodded bravely on
From early morning 'till the day was gone.
We got to Bethlehem by evening light,
I knew the Saviour would be born that night.
We went from place to place in that small town,
In every inn the answer was, "No room."

I was so tired I couldn't lift my head.
I almost didn't hear when Joseph said,
"The owner of this inn has a dry stable
And you may lie down there, if you are able
To find some comfort on a bed of hay."
God's only Son, my babe, was born that day.

I laid the Christ child in the manger there,
He was so little, beautiful and fair.
Even the cattle seemed to stand in awe,
Outside the stable shone a great bright star.
The shepherd's came, His birth by angels told,
Wise men brought gifts, myrrh, frankincense and gold.

So many memories, pictures in my mind.
Our flight to Egypt, 'twas an anxious time.
My babe grew up, a young man, fine and tall,
Almighty God, our Father, planned it all.
His name, Emmanuel, God's Son from birth,
My babe, His Son, the Lord of heaven and earth.

So many memories, joys and sorrows too,
Came with those words, "The Lord has chosen you."
God had His plan, I was His instrument,
An ordinary girl, through whom He sent
His precious Son to save all men from sin.
My Saviour too, all glory be to Him.
~ I have often wondered how Mary felt when Gabriel appeared to her with
God's wonderful message. This poem is the result of such 'wonderings.'

Joseph's Donkey

The little donkey stood there patiently
As Joseph brushed his coat so soft and grey.
The stable here in Bethlehem was bare,
Only the breath of cattle warmed the air,
Mary was resting on a bed of hay
And in the manger stall the baby lay.

The donkey thought of home, his stable there
In Nazareth, behind the open door where
Jospeh did his work as carpenter.
He'd heard him talk to Mary, heard them share
Their plans to go to Bethlehem to sign
The census, Joseph was of David's line.

Joseph had brushed and saddled him that morn,
Mary must ride, her babe would soon be born.
He'd trotted gently o'er the dusty road
Making the journey smoother for his load.
The town was crowded when they reached the gates,
The inns were full, the hour was very late.

The stable of the inn was rough and rude,
The donkey could see all from where he stood.
He heard the wise men call the babe a King,
He saw the shepherds kneel and worship Him.
Of course he'd known, right from the very first
That God had come to live with men on earth.

He knew that Mary's babe was God's own Son
Because God loved the world He had been born,
And that one day upon a tree He'd die
For men and women, such as you and I,
And that Creator God had made all things
To worship Jesus Christ the Heavenly King.

Continued

213

So now they'd have to travel once again.
For God had warned dear Joseph in a dream
That Herod planned to try to kill this child,
This little baby, born so meek and mild.
He'd carry them to Egypt, they'd be safe,
And one day they'd go home to Nazareth.

We accept as "gospel" the idea that Jospeh and Mary
travelled from Nazareth to Bethehem, although this is not
stated in the New Testament. I hope you enjoy this poem
written from the donkey's point of view.

Candles at Christmas

What would Christmas be like without candles?
Have you ever considered the thought?
Are you young enough still to remember the thrill
You got as a child, when you caught your first sight
Of the lights on the tree and the windowsill?

What would we do without candles?
The shadowy glow of the light.
The reds and the blues, the greens and the white,
In clusters on tables they make quite a sight.
At Christmas we'd miss their soft light.

In the beginning, God made the light.
With care He divivided the day from the night.
The sun and the moon, the stars in the sky,
All created in love for man to enjoy,
The light in the world, and the light in man's eye.

But man in his folly brought darkness to earth,
And sin in man's soul meant sorrow and death,
Then God showed His love in a baby's birth,
A star showed the way to the manger stall
Where the Light of the World was born for us all.

So this Christmas time when the candles glow,
Remember the lesson the candle light shows
In the carols we sing, and the joy we bestow,
We are lights in the world to show men the way
To the Light of the World born on Christmas day.

When I think of candlelight at Christmas time I remember
this story. During the 1914-1918 war, people in America,
who had a son killed, put a candle in the window as a sign
that they had given him for their country. A child, seeing
the evening star alone in the sky, was heard to say that God
must have given His Son to die for the world because His
"candle" was shining brightly above.

The Shepherd's Story

Luke 2:8-20

Today I saw the man called Jesus die.
I heard the angry crowd roar, "Crucify."
I saw His mother Mary stand and weep
Beneath the cross on Calvary's hill, so steep.
And memories, undimmed with passing years
Returned to me, and filled my heart with tears.

That night upon the hill was dark and cold.
The sheep were safely gathered in the fold.
My father and my brothers were asleep,
I was on watch, my turn to guard the sheep.
I huddled closer to the dying fire,
And then, my eye was caught by one bright star.

It hung there, low in the midnight sky,
It seemed to beckon me, I wondered why,
And then I heard sweet singing far away,
I looked around, the night was bright as day.
I woke my family and we stared in fear
As angel voices rang out, strong and clear.

One heavenly being, brighter than all the rest,
Spoke to us gently, as in fear we pressed
Closely together on the stony hill.
"Fear not, you shephereds, joyful news I bring
To thrill the hearts of men, now, and in years to come
Glad news, of One, a Baby, born to be King."

The angel told us of a Saviour's birth
That God had come to live with men on earth,
That down in David's city was a stall
Cradling a baby, born to save us all.
The star would show us where the baby lay
In swaddling bands among the dusty hay.

Continued

A multitude of angels joined in songs
Of praise to God, and then departed.
All was still; we looked at one another.
Father said, "Let's go and see the baby
Born today, the shining star
Will guide us on our way."
We reached the stable, rough it was and bare.
I entered first, and saw His mother Mary,
Fair and lovely as she bent over the baby,
Joseph stood by, the scent of cattle
Mingled with they hay. We stood in awe,
And then we kneeled to pray.

So many years ago. I heard of Him,
And saw Him grow from youth to a man and draw
The crowds of needy to His side.
Today I heard the crowds cry "Crucify!"
He was that baby of Whose birth the angels told
That night I kept my watch beside the fold.

Perhaps it is unusual to begin a Christmas poem with a
"picture" of the crucifuxion, but, as Jesus was born to die
on the cross, we cannot separate the two events. I think
that Luke 2:8-20 in the words of the Authorised Version is
pure poetry.

Another Way

Matthew 2:12

Watching the star, the wise men travelled on,
O'er rough and smooth, it led them, far from home.
Long months had passed since first they'd seen its light,
And learned the meaning, heralded by its sight.
A Prince was born, in lands far to the west,
Somewhere in Jewish country, was their guess.

Their journey took them over hill and vale.
Through deserts, sandstorms, pleasant winds and gales,
A baby Prince was born in Israel,
Promised of old, His name, Emmanuel,
A holy child, Messiah come to earth
To save the world; the reason for His birth.

They thought He'd be in royal spleandour laid,
In silken robes, soft blankets for His bed.
But not in royal palace was He found
But in a simple home in Bethlehem town.
They brought their gifts and laid before Him there,
Perfume of frankincense and gold and myrrh.

The star had guided all along the way
To this small child, on this momentous day.
Their hearts were touched with love and joy anew,
Faith in the baby, Jesus the Saviour, grew.
Then, in a dream, they heard God's message say,
"Return now to your homes another way."

The wise men sought and found the Son of God,
The Saviour of the world, Jesus the Lord.
And they returned, rejoicing, day by day.
They took another road, another way.
Life changed for them that day in Bethlehem,
They found the Lord and knelt and worshipped Him.

Continued

When we find Christ, we take another road.
We follow His directions, trust His word.
Forgetting things behind, we reached ahead,
He is our star, we go where we are led.
His presence going with us every day,
As we step out upon another way.

At the beginning of each year many people make New Year resolutions about changing their lives, taking a new way. Usually these self promises are forgotten very quickly. Jesus said, "I am the Way." John 14:6

If Christ Had Not Come

The presents were wrapped, the stockings hung up,
The Christmas tree sparkling, the angel on top.
Garlands were hanging from ceiling and walls
With mistletoe, holly and silver balls.
The logs on the fire gave out glowing heat,
The scents from the kitchen spoke of good things to eat.
I leaned back in my chair and thought of the morn,
'Twould be Christmas day, when the Christ child was born.

I slept and I dreamed I had wakened to see
That the room was all bare, there was no Christmas tree,
No presents, no stockings, the lights had all gone,
No knowledge of Jesus, he hadn't been born.
There wasn't a church outside in the street,
No loving fellowship, no friends to greet,
I went to my study and found, as I feared,
The books about Jesus had all disappeared.

A ring at the door, a small boy stood there
Sobbing and crying about his mother.
Would I come and visit? The woman was ill.
I opened my Bible and sat very still,
For, the gospels were missing, I couldn't give her
A real word of comfort about a Saviour.
No promise of hope, no glory to share
I sat by her bed, head bowed in despair.

Later that week, I stood by her grave
With no word to console, no word that could save,
No resurrection, no glorious heaven
No joyous reunion, no blessing given.
I wept, in my dream, such hot bitter tears,
As I realised then that He was not here.
Christ had not come. He hadn't been born.
There was no Christmas Eve and no Christmas morn.

Continued

I awoke with a start and a great flood of praise
Filled my whole being, for voices were raised
In glorious harmony, there, in my church,
In a beautiful carol I love my much
"O come all ye faithful," the church bells rang out.
My heart lifted in joy, I gave a great shout,
"O come and behold Him, for born is God's Son,
O, come let us adore Him, Christ Jesus has come."

When looking for new ideas for Christmas poems I read
the story, from which I wrote this poem in Streams in the
Desert by Mrs. Cowman. I found the idea very thought-
provoking and the poem was very warmly received during
the 1981 Christmas period.
A few years ago a striking Christmas card was published,
with this title, "If Christ had not come." It was founded
upon the Saviour's words, "If I had not come." The card
represented a clergyman falling into a short sleep in his
study on Christmas morning and dreaming of a world into
which Jesus had never come.

The Star

Matthew 2:2

Darkness fell quickly o'er the land that night,
O'er rugged hills outlined in the evening light.
In Bethlehem the wind howled in the streets,
Crowds hurried home to warmth and food to eat,
All of them busy, none to lift an eye
To where a star shone in the evening sky.
Their doors were closed, no room, no bed to spare
For any stranger late, and none to care.

Way out along the road from Nazareth
A donkey plodded slowely in the dust,
Upon his back, weary, tired, their rode
A woman, and in front a tall man strode,
Leading the donkey gently on his way.
Would they arrive before the end of day?
There, in the sky, a star hung, shining bright
Guiding the weary travellers by its light.

Where would they rest that night, was Joseph's thought.
The crowds had left them far behind; he really ought
To have remembered Mary's plight,
But now, they would arrive late in the night,
Where would he find a shelter for her need?
The shining star above them seemed to lead
Them, would it point the way to where God's Son,
The infant Saviour, Jesus, would be born?

Down in the shepherd's fields, the wind blew cold.
Huddled around the fire, men young and old
Sat in deep thought, while others lay asleep.
Say the bright star as o'er the town it hung.
Heard the swet song by choirs of angels sung,
Listened in awe to news of Jesus' birth,
A Saviour come to live with men on earth.

Continued

Far in the desert kings on camels rode
Eyes following the star, as its light showed
Clear in the night the way the men should go.
A baby King was born, they did not know
That Herod's palace was not where He lay,
But in a stable nestled in the hay.
The holy Child, God's Son, was lowly born.
The star proclaimed His birth that early morn.

Mary and Joseph,the shepherds and the kings
All saw the star and heard it's message bring
Joy to the world, and love and peace on earth,
The wond'rous story of the Saviour's birth.
But as in Bethlehem, so we today
Selfishly busy, do not see the way
The shining star still leads at Christmas tide.
We shut our hearts to those who are outside,
The strangers, lonely, lost for whom Christ died.

Although the star is only mentioned in Matthew's gospel in
connection with the wise men, many others may have seen
it as well. May we all remember the message of "The Star"
when excitement of Christmas has vanished.

The Innkeeper Remembers

I remember well, that evening,
We were busy as could be,
All our rooms were overflowing,
For the Roman census taking,
When our servant said to me,
"There's a couple, with a donkey,
Asking for you urgently."

I remember how, that evening,
When I saw them at the door,
When I had to tell them, "Sorry
There's no room for any more,"
That a great, bright star was shining,
And it seemed to hang right o'er
The rooftop of our stable
And my heart was very sore.

I remember Joseph pleading,
Mary looking tired and worn.
The donkey standing patiently.
My heart was touched and torn
When Joseph whsipered softly,
"Soon her baby will be born,"
I just had to give them shelter
From the bitter cold and storm.

I remember, as I showed them
To the stable in the yard,
That bright star still stood over head
As if it was on guard;
The air was warm inside the stable,
The cattle safely in their shed.
Joseph pulled hay from the manger
And spread it out for Mary's bed.

Continued

I remember clearly also
When the Baby boy was born,
How some shepherds from the hillside
Knelt in worship in the dawn.
Told us of the angels' singing,
Of the message of His birth
Brought to simple men, glad tidings,
Joy to all and peace on earth.

I remember too, that evening
When some wise men from afar
Enquired about the Baby,
Said they'd followed a bright star.
I saw them kneel before Him,
And spread gifts before Him there,
Mary showed them to me later,
Gold and frankincense and myrrh.

I often think, as I remember
All that happened here that night,
That I could have missed the Saviour
If I'd kept the door shut tight.
So, may each of you remember,
As you celebrate His birth,
To open your heart's door to Jesus
That you may know His peace on earth.

Luke 2:7 reads, "And she brought forth her first-born son, and wrapped him in swaddlng clothes, and laid him in a manger; because there was no room for them in the inn." We think of the manger as belonging to the inn and so, for this poem, I thought of the innkeeper taking an interest in the couple, the baby and the happenings of that night.

Easter Poems

The Dying Man

Accounts from the four Gospels

They crowded round the cross, that day He died,
Watching and taunting Him, the Crucified,
Jeering - He'd claimed to be the Son of God,
Laughing - they strained to hear his dying words,
Mocking - the priests and elders turned to gaze,
"Others He saved - Himself He could not save."
And many shouted derisively,
"Come down now from the cross and we'll believe."

No cry of pain escaped the Saviour's lips,
As, spread upon the cross, His hands were split.
The soldiers hammered nails into His feet,
The, sat beneath the cross in all the heat
And gambled for his robe and cursed and swore,
While He, in agony, God's anger bore
For men and dying there, He prayed anew,
"Father, forgive, they know not what they do."

The Saviour saw the women there, below.
His mother knew the sword had pierced her soul.
They stood and gazed on their beloved One,
Mary, in anguish, supported by John's arm.
Jesus knew well how lonely she would be
When He was gone, and from that awful tree
Provided for her care in days to come,
"Mother, your son is John - John, take her home."

That day, two thieves were also crucified
On either side the Saviour as He died.
One of them taunted Him and vilely cursed,
"Aren't you the Christ, then save yourself and us."
The other thief rebuked him, "Don't you fear
God's punishment on us as we hang here?
Jesus, remember me in heaven," he prayed.
You'll be with Me in heaven today," Christ said.

Continued

228

Darkness had fallen all across the sky,
Nature refused man's lust to see Him die.
Darkness indeed enveloped Jesus' soul,
To bear sin's punishment His only goal.
For our transgressions He was crucified,
Wounded and bruised, for us, the Saviour died,
And in the darkness cried, in agony,
"My God, my God, why hast thou so forsaken me?"

The hours passed by, the light returned again.
His body, now exposed in all its pain
Rebelled against the heat, His voice was heard
Fulfilling the predictions of God's Word,
Crying, "I thirst," humanity laid bare,
God manifest in flesh our body shared.
Then one, in pity, dipped into a jar
And gave our Lord a drink of vinegar.

The crowd was quiet now upon the hill,
Uneasy in the heat and dust, until
A shout of triumph echoed through the air,
And, "it is finished," cried the Conqueror;
"Into Thy hands, My Father, I commend
My Spirit now," the Saviour prayed and then
He bowed His thorn-crowned head and died
And death was conquered by the Crucified.

The Stranger

Luke 23:26

The crowds had pushed hi down the narrow street;
Caught in their frenzy in the burning heat,
Not knowing what was happening around.
Simon had struggled to some higher ground
Hoping to see why all the passers by
Were chanting out the one word, "Crucify."
He strained to see above the jeering men
What caused the riot in Jerusalem.

He'd travelled from Cyrene, far away,
To celebrate Passover and pray
And worship in the holy temple here
Among his fellow Jews - now it appeared
Some crisis had arisen to cause outcry,
Even the priests were shouting, "Crucify."
Who did they want to put to death that day?
Only the worst of sinners died that way.

The crowd grew more extreme; much more excited,
Shouting and jeering - now their lines divided,
Simon was appalled by what he saw -
A beaten man - His flesh, bleeding and raw -
Was stumbling, falling, crawling up his back.
He could not see - His blood blinded His eyes -
No sound escaped His lips - no groans, no cries!

Simon could hardly view the awful scene.
The soldiers used their whips, with oaths obscene,
Upon the young man spread there in the road
Unable now, to carry that dreadful load.
They needed someone strong, they looked around,
The stranger - Simon - was the one they found.
Too fearful to resist, he bore that tree
For One he did not know, up Calvary.

Continued

Simon stood, watching, as the young Man died,
He heard His words as He was crucified.
He heard Him pray, "Father forgive their sin,"
As, cruelly, they hammered nails in Him.
He read the writing as the darkness grew,
This man is Jesus Christ, King of the Jews."
And, at the end, he heard the soldier say,
"We crucified the Son of God, today."

The soldiers in Jerusalem compelled
Simon to bear the cross, but he beheld
That wond'rous tragedy,
He heard the last words spoken from the tree;
Because of an apparent accident
Simon was there that day - he had been sent.
And through him many came to know the Lord.
He bore Christ's cross - he met the Son of God.

The Garden

There, in the morning light, the city lay
Golden and gleaming, in the hot sun's rays.
The streets, already packed with busy crowds,
Arabs and Jews, crying their wares aloud.
Gentiles from many lands on pilgrimage
To this, the Holy City, to this stage
On which Jesus, God's only Son was slain,
Buried in Joseph's tomb, and rose again.

Jerusalem's dust streets were filled with noise.
Veiled Arab women, heavy basket poised
On covered heads, went on their way.
Beggars, with outstretched hands, day after day
Lining the filthy streets, and over all
The spicy smells of food on many stalls
Mixed with the fumes of petrol in the air
From cars and buses, racing here and there.

I left the noisy crowds, the busy street,
The beggars, sitting in the burning heat,
And through a door, set in a high stone wall,
Entered a quiet garden where trees, tall
And stately stood, their shadows on the ground
Making cool resting places all around.
A small bird sang, high on a branch, somewhere
Perfume from many flowers, filled the warm air.

I took a seat under a shady tree.
I felt as if the silence spoke to me.
The air seemed holy, full of quiet peace.
It was as though the outside world had ceased
To be and there I sat, in contemplation lost,
For this was Calvary's garden of the cross.
I could see Golgotha, that place of doom
And there, beyond the trees, the empty tomb.

Continued

Wrapped in that beauty, pictures filled my mind.
I heard the soldier's laughter and the grind
Of that great stone they rolled before the door.
Joseph, who owned the garden, stood there too
Head bowed in sorrow; I could see a few
Veiled women, hear their sobs filling the air.
All seemed so real I felt that I was there.

The picture changed again; the mists of dawn
Were cleared away; 'twas early morn
When, through the trees, a weeping woman moved.
I saw her face, its ravaged features proved
Her tears were for the One within the grave.
Then, suddenly, she changed, she looked amazed,
Then puzzled; what wonder and joy lit up her face,
Where that great stone had been was empty space.

Among the trees Another then appeared.
The woman turned about as if in fear,
But some familiar movement caught her eye,
She fell upon her knees, I heard her cry,
"Rabboni, Master, is it really You?"
"Mary," He said, and with those words I knew
That, in imagination, I had been
A silent witness to that sacred scene.

The silence in the garden kept me still
Sitting in contemplation, there, until
It seemed to me, a touch, lighter than air,
More gentle than a breeze, brushed o'er my hair.
I heard my name whispered in loving tones,
"My child, I am alive, and you are not alone,
I rose victorious, from that empty grave
My blood was shed a sinful world to save."

Continued

I left that quiet place, that empty tomb,
I left that golden city, travelled home
To mundane tasks and ordinary ways,
But often, in the passing of the days,
I feel that touch again, hear that dear voice
Speaking my name, "My child, rejoice
In Me." Again He says, in loving tones,
"I've risen, I'm alive, you're not alone."

In August 1980 we spent two memorable weeks in Israel.
The beauty of the garden at Gordon's Calvary, considered
by many Christians to be the true site of Christ's death,
burial and resurrection, inspired this poem.

Mary's Thoughts on Good Friday

John 19:25-27

The room is dark and all is quiet now,
I am alone and lonely in my grief
So much has happened - if my thoughts allow
I'll tell you of my Son - words bring relief
And memories are dear.

What did I think as on that hill I stood
Amid the crowd who'd come to mock and taunt
My Son upon the cross? Their words were rude,
Their faces filled with hate - enough to daunt
The strongest of His friends - and we were weak.

This is my Son, I see Him standing there,
Yet I can't believe that all has come to pass.
The angel Gabriel said a son I'd bear,
Old Simeon said, "A sword shall pierce thy soul," alas
And now it's happened.

I gave Him birth in Bethlehem's stable cold,
The shepherds knelt, and wise men from the east, in worship.
Then came an angel, once again and told us
To flee with Him to Egypt.
Then we went home to Nazareth.

For thirty years I knew Him as my Son,
Yet not mine, He was the Son of God in human frame.
He helped dear Joseph 'till the work was done
Then off He'd go to help the sick and lame,
His thoughts always of others.

We had a wedding once in Cana, Galilee,
He too was there, He loved to join the fun,
The wine ran short, the servants came to me,
I told my Son, He spoke, and it was done.
The wine poured out in love.

Continued

Three short years, He gave to all in need,
His twelve disciples followed in His way,
Love for the Father, love in word and deed,
"Forgive, forgive," was what He used to say,
And now they've silenced Him.

Today I stood and watched Him crucified,
He thought of me and bade John take me home,
"Forgive them, God," He whispered, then He died,
And now I'm here - it's dark and I'm alone
Without my Son.

Have you ever taken the time to think of what our Lord's mother suffered when He was crucified? We know that she stood with the other women at the cross. May I take you, in imagination, into her home on the evening of the crucifixion?

Mary's Thoughts on Easter Sunday

John 20

Three days ago I sat alone and cried,
My Son was dead, the future looked so black.
His friends had scattered, each thought,
"He's dead, I must go back, back to the sea
From where He first called me."

Now all has changed, my heart is full of praise.
We took the spices, early in the morning
Down to the grave and there we stood, amazed.
The stone was rolled away, and in the dawning
An angel spoke to us these words of cheer,
"Fear not, you women, He you came to seek is gone,
He's risen, He's not here."

Yes, He had told us He would rise again,
I should have known they could not kill God's Son.
He showed Himself to us - He looked the same,
Yet not the same, the marks of what was done
Upon His hands and in his side,
He is alive, my Son, my King,
He is alive.

This poem follows the previous one as spring follows winter. Between Good Friday and Easter Sunday the women
and the disciples were in despair, but Jesus rose from the
grave and brought hope, joy and life to them and to all
who through the years, have trusted Him. I hope this poem
gladdens your heart as you read it.

Look Up

It was early dawn when the women came
Bearing the spices toward the tomb.
Their heads were bent in the sorrow of loss,
For their Lord had died on a Roman cross.
Now they came to anoint His body in death,
Their thoughts heavy and sad and their eyes down cast.
"Who will roll the stone away from the door?"
They murmered from hearts which were lonely and sore.

They moved together between the trees,
Their voices were clear in the gentle breeze
"What will we do with that great stone?
We won't be able to move it alone,
It took strong men to place it there.
What will we do? We'd never dare
To ask the soldiers to roll it away.
We'll have to make haste, it will soon be day."

The women moved on towards the tomb,
Their steps unsure in the morning gloom.
Tears blinded their eyes as, with heads bent low
They discussed the events of three days ago.
The arrest, the trial, the death of their Lord
Whom they'd trusted and served and greatly adored.
They lifted their eyes as they reached the tomb.
They could not believe it, where was the stone?

That great big stone had been rolled away.
Their problem was solved in the light of day,
When they lifted their eyes the stone had gone
And with it their fears; they were not alone.
When we lift our eyes from our problems and sins
And look at our Lord, put our trust in Him,
The "stones" in our lives will be rolled away.
So look to the Saviour and watch and pray.

Continued

Mark 16:4 reads, "And looking up they see that the stone is rolled back, for it was exceeding great."

Amy Carmichael says in "Edges of His Ways": The sorrowful women were looking down as they walked. We often do that in sorrow. They were wondering who would roll away the stone. They did not see till they looked up that it had been rolled away.

The Donkey

We bear the mark – the cross upon our backs
Since that one day I never will forget.
I stood at the crossroads at Bethany,
The sun was beating from a clear blue sky,
Some old men nodded in the midday heat
When I saw two strange men walk down the street.
As they approached I knew they'd come for me,
That I was chosen – as they set me free.

The old men called, as they untied my rope,
"Who gave you leave to take away the colt?"
"The Lord has need of him," I heard them say.
The old man smiled as they led me away.
Where were they taking me? I did not know.
In only knew I felt compelled to go.
Someone was calling me, had need of me
And so I went with them - left Bethany.

Excited crowds lined both sides of the road
Awaiting someone - then toward me strode
A Man, Who smiled and gently stroked my head,
"No one has ever ridden you," he said.
"But I have chosen you to carry me
Today along this road from Bethany
Towards a cross upon Mount Calvary
And ever after wear the marks for me."

His followers placed their coats upon my back
And many more were laid along the track
That day I carried Jesus through the crowds,
Who waved palm branches high, and cried aloud,
"Hosanna in the Highest - praise the King.
Hosanna to the King, Who is the Lord.
Hosanna," still they cried, along the road.

Continued

Yes - they hailed Him as their King, that joyous day.
But later in that week they changed their cry
To, "Crucify Him, crucify that man,"
And watched Him die, nailed by his feet and hands,
Not understanding that He was God's Son
Sent to this world, that men might be forgiven
The sin that separates them from the Lord,
'Till they repent and trust the Living Word.

Mary Magdelene

Mark 16:9

Who will roll the stone from my dear Lord's tomb?
Was Mary's thought, as she came, in the early dawn,
To the quiet garden where He had been laid
Three days ago; she was very afraid
As she quietly slipped through the tall, green trees.
What will I do, what will happen to me?
Tears blinded her eyes; "What will I do?" she softly said,
"Now that my Saviour, my dear Lord, is dead."

Mary's thoughts wandered back to that wonderful day
When she'd knelt before Christ on that dusty way.
She'd been plagued with illness, most of her life,
Possessed by devils, by inner strife,
Then Peter had told her of Jesus, the Lord,
Who had healed a young servant, just by speaking a word.
She had met Him, He healed her and set her free,
And now, He was dead, crucified on a tree.

Mary lifted her head as she came to His grave,
Where, where was the stone? She trembled, amazed
That great stone had gone, had been rolled away.
What had happened here? Then she heard a voice say,
"Why seek ye the living among the dead?
Come, see the place where His body was laid,
The Lord is not here, He's risen, He's gone."
Confused and bewildered, Mary turned from the tomb.

Through the garden she stumbled, eyes blinded with tears.
Then a figure appeared from the shadowy trees.
Mary was startled; Who could it be?
A gardener perhaps? Or could it be He?
Could it be Jesus? She fell on her knees.
"Mary," He said. She could hardly believe it.
Her Lord, Who'd been dead, crucified,
Buried there in that grave, now was alive.
She was no longer alone, He'd risen, the whole world to save.
Continued

242

~ Mary Magdalene must have loved the Lord very much and her sorrow and loss brought her to the tomb that first Easter morning. She was rewarded by being the first person to see the risen Lord.

Three Rusty Nails

John 20:25

The nails had lain, forgotten, red with rust,
Hidden from sight, covered in mounds of dust
Upon a shelf, there, on the carpenter's stall
Which stood across the road from Pilate's hall.
They were too big and long for his fine work
And so, they lay there, useless, in the dirt.

The old man saw the crowds passing that day.
They pushed and shoved each other in the way.
He'd heard, the soldiers had arrested Christ
Sometime during the darkness of night.
They'd dragged Him to the High Priest first of all,
And now, He stood on trial in Pilate's hall.

The old man's thoughts were sad and far away,
Recalling how he'd met the Christ one day.
He'd come, with His disciples, up the street,
Wearied by walking, He had found a seat
There, in the shade, beside the old man's stall.
And that was the beginning of it all.

The Christ had spoken as He sat at rest.
Admired his tools, all of the very best
He could afford; a good workman he'd been,
All of his life, a carpenter, keen
To bring beauty from a piece of wood.
He'd prospered; people knew his work was good.

Jesus had lifted a carving of a lamb,
Had held it, lovingly, between His hands.
He'd called Himself, 'the Lamb of God,' that day,
He'd smiled at him and gone upon His way.
Since then, the old man's soul had been at peace
Because he'd met and talked, that day, with Christ.

Continued

The old man's thoughts were broken by a shout.
He saw a Roman soldier running out
Of Pilate's courtyard, straight across the road.
Towards him and his stall he strode,
"I want three nails, quickly, three large, strong nails,"
He shouted at the old man, weak and frail.

With trembling hands, the old man searched around,
Among the dusty shavings, 'till he found
The rusty nails, sharp pointed, very long.
"Just right," the soldier said, "here take this coin,
It surely is enough to pay
To hold that Jew upon His cross, today."

The old man caught the coin the soldier tossed,
Not quite believing him about 'a cross'.
But then, the soldier joked about the nails,
How they would hold a body, without fail.
"Please, let me buy them back," the old man pled,
The soldier laughed and slowly shook his head.

"The crowd has chosen Barabbas, not the Christ,
Listen, they're calling now for Jesus' death."
The soldier went, the old man left his stall
And, trembling, took the road past Pilate's hall,
Along the street and up the stony way,
The path the Christ must take to Calvary.

He hadn't long to wait; he heard their jeers
Long before any of the crowd appeared.
Then came the Lord, dragging the heavy cross,
The soldiers round Him; he was at a loss
To know how best to help his burdened Lord.
How was he going to make Him hear his words?

As Jesus drew abreast of him He stopped,
Unable to carry, further, that great cross.
The carpenter stooped down to wipe His brow,
"I'm sorry Lord – the nails – I didn't know."
His stammering tongue fell silent, as he heard
The Saviour whisper, "I am the Lamb of God."   *Continued*

The nails, which held the Saviour to that tree,
Were nails of sin, driven by you, by me.
Our Saviour turned them into nails of love
As He hung there, praying to God above
For sinners everywhere, for me, for you,
"Father forgive, they know not what they do."
Beside the throne the Lamb of God now stands,
We'll know Him by the nail prints in His hands

~ One Sunday morning when listening to Downtown
Radio's programme 'Reflections', I heard the song 'Three
Rusty Nails' played. I thought that the story would make an
interesting poem. My imagination has embroidered it quite
a bit.

Barabbas

Matthew 27:15-23

He died today, that Man from Galilee.
They crucified Him there on Calvary.
I watched the soldiers nail Him to the cross,
I listened to the women wail their loss,
I saw the darkness creep across the sky
And in my place I saw the Saviour die.

I'd spent my life amongst a band of thieves,
But in my youth, you'll hardly this believe,
John Baptist was my friend, I knew him well,
He was a character, he used to tell
Me I was lost unless I changed my ways,
I should repent and serve God all my days.

I must admit, I thought it was a joke,
Although my friend, he was a funny bloke,
He roamed the hills around Lake Galilee,
He wore queer clothes, ate honey from wild bees,
And taught the crowds they must their sins repent,
Believe in God, and in the One He'd sent.

My friends and I hid out among the hills,
The Romans called us rebels, for we killed
And plundered in the countryside around,
They threw in prison those of us they found.
We recognised no laws but those we made,
Of neither God nor man were we afraid.

One day the news came, Herod had killed John.
He was my friend, whom I relied upon,
It seemed to me I'd nothing left in life
But robbery and killing, sin and strife.
Then I was caught, the sentence passed was death,
I had no hope, no peace, no God, no faith.

Continued

In jail I heard that something was afoot,
The Pharisees and Priests had planned to put to death
Upon a cross the Man called Christ
And have the crowd demand I be released;
Many believe He was the Son of God
The Priests accused Him, calling Him a fraud.

Within my cell I heard the crowd's wild cry,
"Release Barabbas, Jesus crucify"
The soldiers dragged me roughly up the stairs,
A Man was standing, His beaten body bared,
A crown of thorns was jammed upon His head,
His brow was dripping with the blood He'd shed.

The soldiers laid the cross upon His back,
I watched Him drag it up the stony track.
He stumbled underneath the heavy tree,
I reached His side, He turned His gaze on me,
I looked into His eyes, such love was there,
My stony heart was touched, my soul laid bare.

So now, I know, He suffered there for me,
He took my place that I could be set free.
He whispered His forgiveness for my sin,
And from today I've given my life to Him.
And for you too His precious blood was shed,
In love upon the cross your debt He paid.
Oh give your life to Him and you will be
Forgiven, redeemed, by Christ of Calvary.

Pilate's Wife

Matthew 27:19-37

I knew, that day, that something was afoot.
Pilate was worried, rushing in and out
Interviewing Jews, Scribes and Pharisees,
Their priests coming and going secretly.
Rumours were rife here, in Jerusalem,
Conflicting stories spread all about Him,
The Man, Whom all the hubbub was about
Jesus from Galilee, without a doubt.

I'd heard about this Jesus from my maid,
A lovely little Jewish girl, She'd said,
He'd lived in Nazareth for many years,
But lately, He had travelled far and near
Preaching to all about the love of God,
Whom He called Father; many called Him, Lord.
Crowds followed Him and listened to His Words,
Many were healed, blind had their sight restored.

I'd heard so much about this Jesus Christ
That I disguised myself and late at night,
Slipped out, with Miriam, my maid,
And joined a crowd going along the road
To Bethany; and there I heard Him speak
Such words of love to all who came to seek
His help and healing; I was greatly moved.
To me, His claim to be God's Son, was proved.

Now, all these Jews were calling for His death
He'd been arrested, brought here, late at night.
And so, my husband, Pilate, was involved
Because he was the Roman governor.
I'd had a dream, a really bad nightmare
About this holy Man and tried to share
My fears with Pilate but I was too late,
He'd given in, left Jesus to His fate.

Continued

That awful crowd kept crying, "Crucify,
Release Barabbas, send that Man to die."
Pilate gave in and washed his hands of blame.
I watched and listened, feeling very shamed
That Pontius Pilate should have joined with men
Who'd laughed and jeered and beaten Christ and then,
Jammed on His head a crown of thorns and cried,
"Hail, King of the Jews," and had Him crucified.

Pilate put up a sign, 'King of the Jews'
Above the cross on Calvary and refused
To change it when the priests complained,
But now, he walks the floor, nervous and strained,
Knowing, the Man, Whom he condemned to die,
Was Jesus Christ, the Son of God, and that I'd
Warned him but he failed to heed
My words and now, it is too late; the Christ is dead.

My little maid came to me late tonight
Her tears had gone, her face, smiling and bright.
She said that Jesus was alive, not dead.
Many had seen Him, remembering that He'd said
He'd rise again on the third day; and I, a Roman, not a Jew,
Believe that every word is true
But now, what can I do but strive
To help my husband, Pilate, understand, Christ is alive.

His Robe

John 13:1-17

We had gathered all together in that upper room.
It was Passover and Jesus knew that soon
It would be time for His betrayal and His death.
He'd sent us out, that afternoon, to meet, by stealth,
A man, carrying a pitcher full of water in the street.
We followed him, and reached this house and greeted him
With Jesus' words, "Where is the guest room where we may
Prepare for Christ, the Passover today?"

All of us knew that this Passover was going to be
No ordinary meal for our dear Lord and we could see,
During the last few weeks, that He was going through
Some powerful struggle; in His private words to us we knew
That death was in His mind, His death; how could our Lord
be killed?
The very thought was foreign to our minds so filled
With dreams of following Christ to victory
Here on this earth and we, His followers, sharing in His
glory.

We all sat down, we'd had a busy day,
And then, our dearest Friend, our Lord stood up and laid
Aside His robe and took a towel, wrapped it round Himself
And, as we looked at Him in wonder and surprise He knelt
Before each one of us and then began to wash our feet.
He came to me, I couldn't move there in my seat;
"You'll never wash my feet, dear Lord," I rashly said,
As there before me knelt the Son of God with bended head.

My Saviour turned His eyes to mine and I could see
The pain and sorrow in their depths because of me.
"Not my feet only Lord, but hands and head as well,"
"That man is clean," He said, "within whose heart I dwell.
For I have shown you here, this night, that you must do
As I have done, to others, you must follow too,
The path that I, your Master, Friend and Lord have shown.
As servants, follow Me, for you are not alone." *Continued*

The Son of God stood up and took His robe again
As we sat there, wrapped in the silence and the calm
Of thought of this example He had left for us.
We did not know His robe would lie beneath a cross,
Where He would die to save all men from sin and shame.
Show them the only way through suffering and pain,
And so provide another robe for man to wear,
The Robe of Righteousness that all His Sons may share.

The Road to Emmaus

Luke 24: 13-40

We really did not know Him when He joined us
That day we sadly walked down to Emmaus.
We'd seen Him die upon that dreadful cross,
Our thoughts were occupied by our great loss.
We knew He'd said on the third day He'd rise,
But we had seen Him die with our own eyes,
How could He be alive?

That morning, women visited the grave
And ran to the disciples with a tale,
The stone was rolled away, and angels said,
"He's not here, see the place where He was laid."
And John and Peter saw the clothes left there,
The body gone, the tomb, empty and bare.
He could not be alive?

The stranger just appeared along the way
And we discussed the happenings of the day.
He asked us why we looked so sad and full of care,
Our hearts so full of tears, would we not share
Our woe? We told Him all about Christ crucified,
Our hopes He would save Israel denied.
He could not be alive?

And even when He started to explain,
And opened up the scriptures, made it plain
From Moses and the Prophets, He was Christ
Who had to suffer on that awful cross.
We did not recognise our blessed Lord
The Saviour of the world, the Son of God.
How could He be alive?

Continued

When we arrived, He wanted to walk on,
But it was growing late, the light had gone.
We begged Him to come in and share our meat,
And as He broke the bread for us to eat
Our eyes were opened, and we knew the Christ,
And as we stared He disappeared from sight.
He really was alive.

'Tho it was late, we started out again
And joined the others in Jerusalem.
"We knew Him when He blessed and broke the bread.
Our hearts just burned within us on the way
Because He walked and talked with us today.
We know He is alive."

He came to us again, "Peace, it is I,
Look at My feet and hands, for you I died,
These wounds I bore that you might be forgiven,
And some day you will reign with Me in heaven.
Go tell all men the things which now you know,
Go, be My witnesses in this world,
Go tell all, He is alive."

Barabbas and his Friends

Luke 23: 33-43

Barabbas stood and watched as his friends died
There, on their crosses, almost side by side.
The middle cross held Jesus, King of the Jews,
Barabbas stood there, very much confused,
For on that centre cross, where he should be,
Was Christ, the Son of God, and he was free.

He listened to his friends as they hung there,
Their screams and curses filled the sultry air.
Between them hung that figure, quiet now,
A crown of thorns upon His bleeding brow.
The crowds around Him laughed and jeered and scoffed,
"King of the Jews, come down now from that cross."

Barabbas stood there in the waning light
Watching his friends, it was a dreadful sight.
And then, he heard the thief, Matthias, call,
"If you're Messiah, prove it and save us all."
But Jesus, as the taunts and laughter grew,
Whispered, "Father, forgive, they know not what they do."

Then, from the other cross beside the Lord,
Came a rebuke, in slow and pain filled words.
"Have you no fear of God as you hang there?
This punishment is just, what we deserve
For all the evil deeds that we have done,
This Man is innocent of any wrong."

Barabbas listening, heard his friend speak on.
"Jesus, forgive the evil deeds I've done.
In these last moments here before I die
Oh Son of God, remember such as I."
Barabbas listening, heard the Saviour say,
"You'll be with me in Paradise today."

Continued

One of the thieves believed and was forgiven.
In his last moments he was promised heaven.
He met the Lord that day on Calvary,
Barabbas heard and maybe, even he
Found cleansing, in the blood of Jesus, shed
Upon that cross and in Barabbas stead.

Christ took our place upon that cruel tree.
He died, in agony, for you and me.
The thief received forgiveness for his sin
At the last moment, as he turned to Him.
There may be no last moment for you, friend.
No warning when you'll reach your journey's end.
The time is passing swiftly, don't delay,
Come to the Saviour here and now, today.

Index of Poems